FOOTLOOSE

MARK WALTERS

www.gonzo.schule

ISBN 9798356406270

The f-word (as well as the c-word once or twice, though never the n-word) is used liberally through this book; if you have a problem with that, best to f-off now.

INTRODUCTION

"Welcome to Sydney, Australia," the pilot says as the plane lands. It's Friday the 13th of December 2013 — an inauspicious start date if ever there were one — and it's the end of the last flight I'll take. From here to Europe, it's boats and buses, trains and camels, tractors and toboggans …

It's the unknown out there, lying in wait for me. Anything could happen. But the unknown is as likely to be good as it is bad. I'll take the leap, and if I should fall into the chasm, well, at the foot of it might be a bouncy castle and pots of gold.

"Why?" you may ask. "Why the hell bother to travel to Europe without flying?"

And I could come up with something interesting: "You see, since I was a wee lad, about five or six …"

But that would be bullshit. So I'll simply say, "Why not?"

AUSTRALIA

SYDNEY

"A journey of a thousand miles begins with a single step." — so said Buddha, or maybe it was Mao; one of those sorts of guys. My first step (and don't worry, I won't write about every one of them) is towards customs at Sydney Airport, and I'm concerned: "Are you bringing into Australia goods that may be prohibited or subject to restrictions, such as medicines, steroids, illegal pornography, firearms, weapons, or illicit drugs?" the customs card asks me — and yes, I am.

Ticking that catch-all box on the customs card, along with the red flags of not having a return ticket, not having any accommodation booked, and not having a job back home to return to, makes me fear that I may get an overly-personal welcome to Australia. The guy who checks the customs cards does a double-take when he looks at mine, then sends me to lane nine in the customs area. This is worrying: lanes one, two, and three are busy with families, backpackers, and businessmen, and four to eight aren't in use. Nine is empty except for two uniformed officials — a man built like a rugby player and a woman with a face like one.

I tell them, "I've got some anti-histamine pills — strong ones, prescription-only."

They look me up and down, then wave me through without even looking inside my bag. They don't even ask to see the prescription — which is handy, as I don't have one.

I think: *Is that it?* Is it *that* easy to smuggle things into Oz? Into a country where cocaine costs over £150 a gram? If I'd known, I'd have packed kilos of it and used the profits to hire an Aussie to piggyback me to Uzbekistan.

I ride a train from the airport to Sydney Central Station and find a hostel near it called Bounce, where I chat with a Welshman, Nathan. I tell him my plan to travel to Europe without flying and that I've packed little for the trip. For footwear, I have only plain, black, rubber flip-flops — the pinnacle of footwear evolution. Comfortable, waterproof, cheap. Plus, you don't have to waste money on socks.

He says, "You haven't got a towel? Or shorts? Or trainers?" He laughs. "That's tickled me, that has. I'll look out for you on the news: 'British tourist with only a toothbrush found dead in the outback'."

When you travel this far — to the far side of the earth — you think things will be different: an unintelligible language — scrawls, probably, like a toddler's — and food that looks regurgitated (eaten if not with the hands then at least with chopsticks), and maybe pyramids or giraffes or pixies. Yet as I wander the streets after I unpack — which takes a couple of minutes; a benefit of travelling like a tramp — to stretch my legs and get a feel for the city, I think, This is just like England; there's a familiarity about it, an inescapably British feel. London feels close more than far. Here could, indeed, be mistaken for a corner of it, and I wouldn't double-take if I saw Potter and his ginger mate walk past on their way to Platform 9¾, about to embark on another year of trying to get Watson to hold their little pink wands. The names of the streets — Elizabeth and Albion — and the names of the parks — Hyde and Belmore. The noble facades of the dignified buildings. The driving on the left of the road. Only the heat — over thirty degrees — and the slim, smiley, tanned people reveal that London this isn't.

They're related, of course, Sydney and London, and not all that distantly. London once upon a time gave birth to

Sydney, and I might share a great-great-grandfather with someone on this street — the same blood might run through our veins. Until 1949, Australians and Britons were, in fact, one and the same. Until then, Australian citizenship didn't exist. A woman born in Sydney was as British as the Queen. Now, with their optimism, and their willingness to smile at strangers in the street, Australians perhaps are more like Americans, but an Englishman will always be half at home here, and I don't feel altogether abroad.

I visit Hyde Park Barracks; in the 1800s, it housed convicts sent to Sydney from the UK. (A lot were sent: 165,000 in total to Australia.) Records stuck on walls show that the British sent most here for minor crimes. Patrick Conaghan, a twenty-five-year-old sailor, received a sentence of seven years in Australia for stealing a cow. If that were the punishment for nicking one, I'd not have gone within a dozen metres of a cow — to be on the safe side, in case anyone thought I might take it. How times have changed. Someone in the UK arrested for stealing a cow these days would be let go the same day. That's if the police even took the incident seriously:

"Hello, officer. A terrible, terrible crime has occurred. It's Daisy; she's been taken."

"Sir, don't worry, we'll find her. Where was she when she was taken? At home?"

"Oh, no, I never let her in the house; she'd defecate everywhere; big, steaming ones she does. No, officer, she was in a field."

"And this field, what was she doing there? Taking a walk?"

"Standing mainly, eating the grass."

"Grass?"

"Yes; she loves it, she does; that's all she eats."

"So she's a vegetarian; I've made a note of that. And, Daisy, what does she look like?"

"She's black and white."

"What's that? Black *and* white?"

"Yes, that's right."

"Err, ok. So, erm, you mean, she's mixed-race?"

"Her race? Oh, I'm not sure about that; but I think she might be from Holland originally."

"Dutch — I'll write that down. And anything else I should know? Distinguishing features?"

"She has large udders."

"Sorry, did you say udders?"

"Yes, that's right. Like, *very* big — a real handful."

"Do you mean, erm, err, she has large breasts?"

"No, officer, I mean udders."

"Sir, is Daisy a cow?"

"Yes, officer."

"Sir."

"Yes."

"You're under arrest."

"What? Me? But I didn't—"

"Yes, you, you fool, for wasting police time. Do you think *I*, do you think *anyone*, gives a toss about a damn cow? Do we hell. You're coming with me."

Seven years on the arse of the earth was the punishment for all sorts of crimes, but the term is slightly misleading, as few had any chance of ever being able to pay their way back at the end of it. It was thus, in all but name, a life sentence. Convicts were housed at Hyde Park Barracks rather than in prison because there weren't any prisons. Pubs, bookies, and brothels were higher on the list of construction priorities — which is understandable. And, anyway, there was no worry about them escaping: Where would they go? Almost certain death awaited anyone who fancied chancing the uncharted wilderness. Their sentence was work-based — sunrise to sunset for no payment. Not hard labour for the sake of it; not just digging holes then filling them in again. There were homes to build, and roads and bridges, and convicts did the constructing. It was their slogging that kick-started Sydney's ascent from huts and tents to the city today that sparkles.

It wasn't all convicts on those boats. Of about a thou-sand-or-so of the first to come, more than half were convicts; the others actually signed up to start a colony on the under-side of the globe. What they found didn't exactly match up with the brochure. They'd been sold a distant, sunny Eden, an England-On-Sea; well, it was distant and sunny and by the sea ... The heat was like nothing in England. Nor the wildlife, a lot of which was severely murderous. And there were no apples on the trees and no berries to pick. As for the natives, well, they kept throwing spears at their newly-arrived neighbours. Everything was against them, those settlers. But they stayed and made the best of it. And this wasn't because of some great British braveness, that Bulldog spirit that had seen the country conquer the world, that stiff upper lip ... No, none of that; they just had no choice. The fast planes and cheap tickets of today make the world seem not so big — I'm about to put that to the test — but it had taken those people 252 days to arrive at Australia (and 25 had died on the way). They couldn't simply mooch around complaining, then write a one-star review on TripAdvisor (AWFUL place! Spiders everywhere and the locals speak NO English!!!) and go home. It was live here or die here, and living is for most people generally better than dying.

From there, I walk through the Royal Botanic Garden: tweets and squawks, flowers yellow and white, red and violet; pot-bellies jogging, office workers on their lunch break; picnics and yoga. And a world-class view, the view that says, *Welcome to Sydney, baby!*: the Opera House, with its multi-peaked, curved, white roof; the imperious Harbour Bridge, its stone towers and graceful steel arch; and spangly skyscrapers clustered around the harbour, where yachts and ferries cross the wake-frothed waterway.

I stroll down to the water to see the Opera House, the city's most famous building. It's far more than just a place for obese fellas to yodel; it's Oz's talisman, Australia emblemised; it's Big Ben, it's Eiffel Tower, it's Statue of Liberty ... And it's shit. It's like going downstairs on Christmas morning to find your parents have bought you Ken instead of Action Man. From a distance, it's iconic, yeah; but up close, it's small and faded and dated. With its dirty tiles, bare concrete underside, and brown-and-yellow pebbledash floor and walls, it looks like a leisure centre built in the seventies. Still, it's an improvement on what once stood at this spot: a tram garage. And it gave Sydney something — anything — unique, at a time when it offered nothing beyond mediocrity and a big bloody bridge. When Melbourne was awarded the 1956 Olympics, Sydney was pissed — "Why not us? We've got a bridge and ... Did we mention the bridge already?" A big fuck-you to their upstagers, that was what they'd need; a thing so magical, so glorious, that from then on no one would award so much as a picnic to Melbourne; something that was at least better than that garage stinking out the waterfront. And thus the Opera House was born — two decades later. Eugene Goossens, head of the Sydney Symphony Orchestra, was its cheerleader, the bloke who got the project underway. Sadly, he never saw his brainchild consummated. He didn't die, no, so put away that tissue — advice that would have served Eugene himself well. When landing at Sydney Airport, customs officials — who back then must have been stricter than they are now — found sordid erotica in his bags. Ruined by the scandal, he returned to Europe in disgrace, never again to set foot in Oz.

I catch a bus to Bondi Beach, where are stores named Earthfield and Abode, and the Tan Temple — "Because you look better brown" — and denim-shorted women in over-sized sunglasses licking ice creams and sipping fresh-pressed juices. Lycra-clad exercisers pound along the prome-nade, and to the beats of drum'n'bass, shaggy-haired, shirt-less dudes flip tricks on BMXs and skateboards. A kilometre of golden sand stretches along the Pacific Ocean; foamy surf rolls onto the curved beach. On the soft sand, games of cricket, of frisbee, and toned, bronzed bodies lazing. Hundreds of surfers in the sea. Some pull off cool moves; others — tourists who have underestimated how hard surfing is — spend the afternoon being tossed around and half-drowned. I wait around hoping to see a shark attack, my hopes buoyed by a conversation with a bloke at the hostel: Dave from Bournemouth told me he's part of the Barmy Army, fans that support the England cricket team; he went to see England play Australia in Adelaide last week, and he and his twelve friends had all bought shark costumes to wear. He said, "But a few days before the match, there was a big news story about a teenager eaten by a shark. I thought it would be bad taste to wear it, so I instead went dressed as a hot dog."

Impatient after an hour, I ask one of the lifeguards if they get many sharks here.

"Yeah, mate," he says. "We've had a few great whites here in the last month. Two were caught in the shark net that's half a kilometre out. The other one, some of the guys got on jet skis to scare it off."

Back at my room — I say "my" room, but there are eight of us in here — some Aussie girls are getting ready for a night on the town — "... Oh my God, oh my God, oh my God ... Do I look like a slut in this dress? ... Let's get those guys upstairs to buy us drinks ..." — and there's a spectacled, spotty lad stood over two open suitcases filled mostly with Lego, but also other toys, like cars and action figures. He spots me staring and says, "I know, I'm crazy. But it's my Lego collection, and I need it. I'm moving to the US to live with my girlfriend, and there's no way I'm leaving it behind." He should be more worried about going through customs in America than I was about going through customs here. He'll get locked up by a shouty man with a crew cut: "You're planning to blow up our asses with a Lego bomb. We know it, boy, and we'll get you to say it. Private Johnson, get the torture room ready. I mean the, err, what are we calling it these days? Enhanced interrogation room? No? We changed it again, did we? Ah, right: American massage therapy suite."

For dinner, I eat Heinz beans in cheesy sauce — reduced in Woolworths to £0.52. I'd eat them cold, right out of the tin, but others here are cooking bolognese and Stroganoff, and I don't want to seem uncivilised, so I pour them into a bowl first. Then I join a bar crawl run by the hostel: A load of us head out to do the rounds, but my night gets cut short when five of the group are denied entry to the club: me for wearing flip-flops; four other guys for being "too old", despite only being in their forties. As I walk back to the hostel with the doddery geriatrics, the injustice of the discrimination simmers within: Have we made no progress? Things must change! I have a dream that our children will one day live in a world where they will not be judged by the style of their footwear but by the content of their character. I have a dream that one day, down in Sydney, flip-flopped boys and flip-flopped girls will be able to join hands with shoed boys and shoed girls as sisters and brothers and party in harmony, as one. I have a dream.

About 3 am, I wake to an odd noise. I look down from my top-bunk with bleary eyes and see Legolad stood swaying. Nathan, also in a top-bunk, looks down and says, "Mate, what are you doing?"

A mumbled reply.

Nathan says, "Are you taking a piss?! For fuck's sake, you filthy fucker."

The noise stops, then Legolad falls back onto his bed. It goes quiet, but Nathan's restless. First I hear him sniffing, then his lighter flares up; he waves it around, searching. And he finds what he hoped not to find: a big pissy patch on the floor in the middle of the room. For a crime like that, it's fair to send him to a far-off land for seven years.

ADELAIDE TO COOBER PEDY

I took a train from Sydney to Melbourne — an eleven-hour ride through prosperous, provincial, prosaic towns that were neat and trim, through fields and hills, past cows and sheep and horses. There are long-standing arguments over which is Australia's premier city; neither Melbourne nor Sydney, though, is the capital. Canberra is, even though it was an obscure farming town when that crown was placed. Why Canberra? Because it's located roughly between the other two and to prevent whoever wasn't picked starting a civil war. Melbourne, I thought, was much like Sydney — minus the Opera House and the big bloody bridge — and the two are about the same size (4.5 million people, give or take a few hundred thousand). It was, in fact, nicer, cleaner, friendlier than Sydney, which had a surprising number of drunks drinking from brown paper bags, addicts and beggars and homeless, for somewhere consistently ranking in top-ten lists of the best cities in the world. I thought: Maybe, each morning, a van drives around Melbourne, and any undesirables are bundled into it and driven to its rival Sydney. When somewhere finally lets me be mayor, that's what I'll do. The key to success is branding: Frogmarching wasters into a white van with SCUM written on the side is a no-no — it would send Twitter into a frenzy. Better to use an ice cream van and operate under the pretence of handing out free Ben & Jerry's to the needy.

"Hey, hob—, err, honoured member of society, would you like a free ice cream?"

"Uh? Who the fuck are you?"

"I'm the mayor."

"Then why are you in an ice cream van?"

"Just out doing good deeds, being a man of the people. So, an ice cream, you want one?"

"Beer, give me a beer. Or a quid so that I can buy a beer."

"We've got *rum* and raisin ice cream."

"Rum, you say? Yeah, then; give me one."

"Ok, my friend, you'll have to come into the van to get it."

"Why? Why can't you just give me it?"

"You have to, erm, sign for it."

The hobo enters the van, and I hand him his ice cream. "Now, just sit there a minute while I find my pen. It's here somewhere." I hunt around a little bit, looking for a pen that's in my pocket. "How's your ice cream, my friend? Like it?"

"It tastes kind of odd. I taste the rum, but not the raisins, and it also tastes of something else. A kind of strange taste that I can't quite place."

"That will be the Rohypnol."

"The what?"

"Rohypnol."

"*Rohypnol?!* You said rum and *raisin*."

"Did I?"

"You definitely didn't say fucking Rohypnol."

"Oh, well, never mind now. Look, you have a little sleep, and by the time you wake up, we'll be in Leeds."

"Sod that — Leeds?! I don't want ... Zzzzzzzzz."

In Melbourne, I went to the train station to book tickets to take trains up to Darwin on the north coast of Australia, where I can get on a boat of some sort — like a yacht if I can blag my way onto one — to Asia. But the clerk at the station told me that trains on that route — which are primarily for freight, not passengers — run only twice a month, and it being Christmas, they're on a break. So lots of bus rides instead. I hate buses. They're a shite way to travel. They take ages, and you're in with the worst of society. It's the mode of transport favoured by drunks, paupers, and — worst of all — backpackers. I'm a backpacker, and I wouldn't want to sit next to me.

It won't be the last obstacle or detour I'll have to face — the road ahead will no doubt be filled with them. But if you're not in a hurry, almost anything is possible; you can go anywhere, do anything. It just takes time.

So I rode a bus to Adelaide, where I've spent a couple of days. It's pretty crap, no Sydney or Melbourne. I saw the "world's biggest rocking horse". It's big — I'll give them that — but it doesn't look like a horse, and it no longer rocks. They've kept the title only due to the total absence of competition. Dubai could better Adelaide's effort in a day if they could be arsed with it.

Now I'm at the bus station — blue-and-silver tinsel above the service desks, big silver stars hung from the ceiling, wreaths above the bus bays — waiting for the Greyhound to Coober Pedy, an arbitrary stop-off on my bus marathon up through Australia's abdomen.

It's a tense moment at a station when the other passengers are assembling. *Which will be on my bus? Who will I be sat next to?* It's like a blind date, but even worse: to bail on a date is as easy as saying you're going to the bathroom then fleeing from a fire escape; but on a bus, a bus in this country, where a journey can be, and often is, twelve hours or more, well, to bolt from your busmates means to get off in Bumblefuck, and wait there a day for the next bus. And unlike a blind date, there's no sexy carrot dangling. Ever shagged anyone you've met on a bus? No. No one has.

I watch the people congregate around me, waiting to board: The guy with a paper, talking to himself: "What a load of crap this is ... Look at this wanker ..." The large woman, red-headed, rough as a dog, with a pushchair and a five-year-old holding a Transformers pillow. She wears jogging bottoms. One inch of arse crack shows when she bends. She sings along to a rap song: "I was walking down the street with my dick in my hand, I'm a cool motherfucker ..." Then stops to yell at her son: "Get your fucking spoon off me, you pig." The six-foot-five blue-eyed, blond-bearded, space cadet in a stained t-shirt and shredded jeans who shuffles stuff around in his bag without making any progress — partly because he keeps stopping to take long, blank stares into the distance. The young child who recites the alphabet then uses a window as an Etch A Sketch: spits on her fingers to scrawl her name then slobbers on her hands to wipe it clean before drawing a crap cat. The big, blunt aboriginal grunting in English; her melon boobs droop down to her stomach. She's just one of many aboriginals — a third of the passengers. The haggard woman in a checked dress; a walking stick and a double-fat ass and a wart on her nose. The unshaved, covered-in-dirt guy, who carries a rusty metal case ...

But I get lucky with two seats to myself — for now.

The driver, for some reason, is dressed like a schoolboy: shorts and a white-collar shirt; pulled up white socks and black brogues. The PA doesn't work, so he has to shout down the bus: "We have a comfort stop in two hours, so try to hold back the heavy artillery. Have some consideration as the air circulates around the whole bus."

Adelaide to Port Augusta first. Out the window, a light blue sky with wispy streaks of white; yellow fields stretch to the horizon, and on hills are wind turbines. The scenes beautiful, to the soundtrack of a bullshit Eddie Murphy movie on four dropdown screens; no headphones, the volume loud. And the red-headed, rough dog and her kid are sat in front of me; he plays a game on a cheapo tablet — a riot of beeps; acid in my ears. Then he starts crying. "Shut the fuck up, Noah," his mum says. "You're going to get smacked out in a minute."

That kid — bad as I feel for him — is actually a little brat. Earlier, he turned around and looked at me, knocked on the window, and laughed. I smiled and knocked on the window, and he laughed. I did this a few times to entertain him. Then he kept turning around and doing it, expecting me to do the same like I'm some kind of window-knocking monkey. When he saw I was out of the game, he burped in my face.

I thought, for revenge, to reveal the Santa hoax: "If Santa were real, he'd be in prison. Gifts to sit on his lap? Elves he doesn't pay a wage? He's a paedo running a sweatshop."

But then I thought I'd give the kid a break: His life is tough enough already.

From Port Augusta, onto the Stuart Highway, full speed down the two-lane road, a smoothly paved highway. The traffic thins from little to nearly none, but now and then lorries and tankers race full at us; some multi-trailered, fifty metres long — so-called road-trains — which haul freight up and down the country. At these speeds, with no central reservation, only a slight twitch from either driver would result in tragedy. The road is unfenced; roaming kangaroos and sheep are a risk, and we at times slow to let animals cross the road.

No towns now. Just the road, the road unrolling to the horizon. Australia is, after all, scarcely inhabited. A population of 23 million in an area 50% greater than Europe. Per square kilometre, Australia has on average 3 people. The USA? 32. And the UK crams in 257. But even Oz's 3 is skewed massively, as over three-quarters of Australians live in the same corner of the country, in the south-east, where Sydney and Melbourne and a few other cities are. In huge swathes of the country, there's no one; it's empty. Along the Stuart Highway, the only vein that pumps through the country's centre, the towns are spread sparsely. Between Port Augusta and Alice Springs, 1,200+ km apart, the Greyhound map I have shows just four towns: Pimba, Coober Pedy, Kulgera, and Erldunda. I Googled them back in Adelaide: Pimba, Kulgera, and Erldunda, each of them is home to less than fifty people. With 1,500 people, Coober Pedy is a whopper by comparison.

As the land grows starker — the onset of Australia's searing desert, it's outback — for an hour, I watch the light retreat from the sky; a spread of colour comes: light blues and bright blues, pink and deep crimson and majestic oranges. Such a vivid sunset, seriously sci-fi, such as I've seen never before. Then stars begin to blossom in the blackness; a million of them, it seems.

I stare into the darkness, the starry night, and think about being on a bus with people I don't know, heading to a town I don't know, at a time when most are home to spend Christmas with loved ones. Few are willing to be away from home at Christmas, seeing it as a sacred event that can't be missed. It's not that special, though; it happens every year, and it's mostly the same every year. If you miss one or two or six, it's no big deal. It's, in fact, good to miss a few: the ones you skip give you a greater appreciation for those that come in the future. It brings back the novelty, which gets lost after going through the same routine annually — gifts, turkey, charades. As for an Australian Christmas, no thanks. In Sydney, in Melbourne, I saw carol singers, I saw a Salvation Army brass band playing *Silent Night*, I saw Christmas puppet displays in the windows of department stores. Yet it didn't feel Christmassy. The locals have done their best, put up trees and decorations, but it's too warm, too light. People in sunglasses and shorts, not scarves and coats. It feels false and futile, like your local boozer trying to pull off an Ibiza club night vibe by stringing up some fairy lights and playing a Daft Punk album.

A half-hour stop at a middle-of-nowhere roadhouse, a petrol station with a diner: a stale, bare room with light brown walls and a cheap, sticky vinyl floor. "Truckies specials": The food all fried crap, cooked hours ago and left to sit. "Dunnies", as the sign calls them: minging toilets, no locks. If you got left behind, you'd be buggered, stuck here until the next bus comes through tomorrow; so some never get off the bus; it's a risk not worth taking for this. A minute too long on the bog ... I do use it, as it's hard to piss straight in the toilet at the back of the bus; half ends up on the floor. It's so tight-spaced, seemingly designed for a Japanese midget child. I'm slim, and I find it hard to manoeuvre — and it's not like I'm trying to dance in there; just do my piss, that's all, yet I have to contort like a crusty sadhu.

Soon after, a stop again; not to get gas: the driver goes to open a padlocked, faded red box and takes out a parcel; he puts the parcel in the hold, and then we drive on. It seems we double-up as a postal service, as we later pull off the main road by a dark, spooky building, and off the driver walks with a package. After ten minutes, he's still not back. Late in the outback, stranded on a bus: it could be a setting for a horror movie. I look about the bus, think who's the most likely murderer. That unshaved, dirty guy, I think, the one I saw put a big, rusty metal case in the hold; he's the one. I'll keep an eye on him. I've no knife, but I've a lighter and spray-on deodorant at hand in my bag: I'll flamethrower the fucker.

Someone should have done that to Ivan Milat, Australia's most notorious killer, who killed at least seven between 1989 and 1993. His nickname: "The Backpacker Murderer". Easy targets are backpackers, naive and often alone. An offer of help from a kind local? *How nice those Aussies are. Yes, please.* Next thing you know, you're tied up, his dick is up your arse, and by morning you're dead in a ditch. Unless you strike first, char his ass.

Hours later — fuck knows where; another marooned roadhouse — I get off the bus to stretch my legs. The rusty-case guy talks to me. His eyes light up when I tell him I'm going to Coober Pedy. "Me too," he says. "I live there." Back on the bus, he sits next to me. I want to sleep — at least try to sleep — but he won't take my yawns as hints. Ash, his name is, a plumber, mid-forties, and he's saying to me, "Coober Pedy is the real Australia; you'll see what it's all about." The real Australia, I think: that doesn't sound good. When most people talk about the real parts of their country, they mean the bits that no one goes to for good reason. In the UK, they mean Norfolk or they mean Liverpool; in short, they mean places where live the poor and the inbreds. "Used to be a big town for mining, but not much now," he tells me. "Dying out, it is. But we still hope for a big find. There's a £400,000 rock in a safety box in Adelaide. I bet some Arab will buy it to put his toothbrush on." He talks and talks, about mining, about aboriginals, about everything and nothing. He tells me about two Germans who died near Coober Pedy after their car broke down. One stayed with the car, and the other went to look for help. "Damned if you do, damned if you don't, eh?" he says and grins at me. They signed a safety sign-in/out book at the pub before leaving; however, their entry was the last one on the book's last page. A replacement book was brought out, meaning that no one noticed they didn't check back in.

"Look," he says, "why don't you stay with me in Coober Pedy?"

I tell him I'll think about it but think to myself that there's no way I will. To go to a small town in the outback and stay with a stranger met on a bus is a story that I fear will end with me getting an axe to the head and being tossed down a mine.

COOBER PEDY

I wake to a pinky-blue sky, a sky over what seems not of this earth. The soil red, eerie, Mars-like; a vast, cruel space, stubbled nothingness, from an awful epoch passed, forged by a savage maker angry at man. The land scraped, scarred. Just rocks scattered, clumps of brittle shrub. No trees, no homes, no nothing. A boundless, barren blank.

And then, hours later, in the distance, Coober Pedy.

The bus pulls into town; the place is dead. Ash still insists that I stay with him. His Filipino wife turns up in a battered pickup truck — all its mends and patches showing, repainted bumps and scars. He opens the truck door for me. "Come on, mate," he says. "It's Christmas. What the heck else are you going to do?!"

It's a good point. My options are limited. And he wouldn't murder me at Christmas, would he?

He's less likely to, at least.

Their home is a shack-like bungalow with a concrete floor throughout. "Costs a hundred bucks a week," Ash says. Three bedrooms — two used to store junk and tools. Out the back — the backdoor is always unlocked, he says — is a small, sandy yard, in which stands the rusted frame of a pig stable that adjoins a barn filled with more junk and tools. A dozen chickens and a rooster roam. When Ash starts chasing the chickens, the rooster attacks him; it leaps in the air and tries to claw him. Ash's Labrador Brick jumps in, barking and snapping. The rooster attacks the dog too.

When the rooster pauses for a second, Ash grabs it and throws it onto the roof of the bungalow.

Ash takes me on a tour of the town, a dreary place in a desolate, derelict setting: the red, rocky desert decorated with abandoned machinery and mounds of dug-up dirt. A couple of decades ago, he tells me, the town boomed on the back of opal mining, but as opal finds dried up and the price of the stone tanked, few had reason to stay. I'm introduced to some who did. Mick lives in a self-built house in a cave and pines for the pre-9/11 days when you could buy dynamite without a licence. Debs manages a subterranean hotel that was once a mine and has an extensive collection of opals — some priced at more than £10,000 — that she can't sell. Tony lives in "the bush" and wears threadbare boots that don't match.

We stop at an off-licence for beers. I have to show ID; not because of my age — a grey hair or two I have — but because people can only have one "slab" — as they call them; a crate of beers — per day. At £27 for twenty-four small cans, alcohol is more expensive in Australia than in any other country I've been to. Cigarettes too: £12 a pack. Chocolate is also taxed to the max. A bar costs £1.50 — twice as much as in the UK. That's the way to stop folks eating unhealthily: skyrocket the price. If a family-sized Toblerone cost £27, our obese friends would think twice before they scoffed the whole lot in one go.

Ash tells me the reason for the one-slab-a-day rule is the "abos" — as he calls them. There are scatterings of aborigines around Coober Pedy, as there were in Sydney and Melbourne, in Adelaide and in between. On the edge of the frame, typically, shadows in the streets and plazas and parks. I've seen few with jobs: in shops or restaurants, in uniforms or suits. Which is odd, as they make up 3% of Australia's population. Lots I've seen are drunks and hobos, look wrecked by booze, drugs, life; they shuffled around, swigging or begging. Even those on the buses seemed not quite right, like they were off in their own world. At them I've smiled and nodded, as I do to all sorts of people I meet, and say hey, or alright, or how's it going, but none have returned any greeting — except those who then asked for money. I saw white ruined people as well, homeless and struggling, but the majority by far were aboriginals.

The coming of Captain Cook just over 200 years ago, in 1770, that for most people is the beginning of Australia, but the original owners of Australia, the aborigines, were here for 60,000 years prior. Thus, aboriginals had the land to themselves for the first 99.5% of Australia's inhabited history. Then came the whites and stole it. That's like you living in a house for twenty-five years, then one day a random kicking your front door in and saying, "You, get out of your house — now. I'm moving in with my mates today. No, I'm not paying you for it, but don't worry, I'll let you have a corner of the garden to sleep in. Keep the noise down, though. If you make too much noise, I'll punch you in the face." 60,000 years is a long time. What they did for all those years is mainly a mystery: When Cook came, these inscrutable locals wore no clothes, sowed no crops, built no houses; there was nothing permanent about their lives. Almost nothing, actually; the only definite achievement — other than survival, which is no small thing in Australia — were huge shell mounds that reached as high as ten metres and were often inland and on hills. So a long culture, but one that seems to involve sitting at its core. No bad thing, I think, for idling is underrated. It's a virtue, to my mind, not to be vilified as it is by civilised society. Time you enjoy wasting is not wasted time, as a wise man said. And left alone, they were happy, these natives. Cook wrote: "They may appear to some to be the most wretched people on earth, but in reality they are far happier than we Europeans ... All they seem to want is for us to be gone."

On the bus here to Coober Pedy, two got off in the middle of nowhere, just out there in the outback — into that desert, that darkness. Not to change buses — they lived there, in that forbidding vacuum. To the east were Sydney and Brisbane. To the south were Melbourne and Adelaide — didn't they know they could live next to the world's biggest rocking horse? Even Coober Pedy, surely that would be preferable to being out there, out in that startling emptiness. But, says Ash, "They've got well-run communities out there — no booze. Those guys are nice, friendly, respectable.

They don't want your money. They prefer to live in their own way. The pain-in-the-arse ones in the towns, they're the dregs; walked away from, or been kicked out of, their communities." So it seems for the majority the choices are two: stay in the sticks and prosper, or go to the likes of Melbourne or Sydney and sink. They can be themselves out there, in that blank wilderness — a wilderness to them that is tame. Cities, on the other hand, are confusion, are foreign, are snake pits. Better to be at peace in the bush, they think, than an alien in a world unknown.

And talking of aliens, Tony is now; they built the Pyramids, he's telling me, as we drink XXXX in Ash's backyard, perched on upturned milk crates under thirty-degree sunshine, fending off flies that buzz at our ears, our eyes. Tony's just back from a two-hour walk, which Ash says is quick for Tony: "Last time he said he was going for a walk, no one saw him again for nine months." Tony's sure about the aliens and the pyramids, but his fifteen-minute tangent doesn't change my mind. I tell him, "The Egyptians: they built the pyramids, slaves did it," but I can't change his mind too. Tony — or Tony the Swag as Ash calls him; a swagman being a kind of Aussie drifter, a hobo — is a curious character: those odd boots, his holey checked shirt and too-tight blue shorts, his straggly beard on his weather-beaten face. I took him to be mid-fifties, but he's actually into his sixties — he's not quite sure of his age beyond the decade — so whatever he's doing out there, he's doing alright by it. Dates aren't a strong point: "I don't have a watch or a calendar," he says. "I didn't even know it was Christmas until Ash told me."

He says, "It's better living out in the bush; less to worry about. When it's dark, I go to bed; when it's light, I wake up; when I'm hungry, I eat."

I ask what he does for food.

He says, "There's loads out there if you know your way about the land. I shoot emus, rabbits, kangaroos. An average-sized kangaroo lasts me a week."

Ash and Tony — who sometimes go out together with pickaxes to look for opal — discuss places to go digging.

I ask how they know where to look for it.

Ash says, "Truth is, it's total luck. You may as well take

your hat off, close your eyes and spin around, and throw the hat as far as you can. Wherever it lands is as good a place to dig as any other. I've got mates who swear by certain strategies, but every one of them has a scrapheap of a motor, so I call bullshit on their strategies."

I say isn't it unlikely that they'll just happen across a good find, that surely all the stuff worth finding has been found, claimed by the mining companies? No, he says; still swathes of the country are uncharted. At least not properly surveyed. They know where all the land is and have satellite images, but no one's walked around most of it taking samples. That infinite expanse, barbarous and baking, no one quite knows what's out there. Fortunes, maybe, just waiting to be found. "Now and then, it's on the news," he says. "Some fella out in the bush with a metal detector, and he finds a big gold nugget, just lying in the desert, and it's worth hundreds of thousands." He tells me another story of a guy in the 1950s who found the world's largest deposit of iron ore: "This guy, Hancock, found it by accident, and, just like that, became a billionaire."

These days, Australia is one of the world's biggest exporters of minerals and metals: coal, zinc, gold, copper, uranium, diamonds, and all sorts of other stuff. A couple of hundred thousand are employed in the industry, and at the hostel in Melbourne, I met one who works in a mine. Slovan, his name was, and his face was fucked after a surfing accident in which he'd banged his face off a rock. His left eye was freaky and bloodshot; his cheekbone was broken. He was on a break from his mine work, which he told me about: his 4 am start time, being underground the whole day, living like a mole. I said that didn't sound much fun, and he told me about it not being uncommon for people to quit after a week or even a couple of days. He told me about him sticking it out so he can save £20,000 to travel afterwards, about his plan to buy a van and drive the whole coast of Australia, then go to Asia for a year. Not a bad plan, I thought, if you can hack that life for a year, and I thought whether this bloke maybe couldn't, as he spent his days at the hostel drinking, often in the bed he'd walled off with a sheet and a towel. The room stunk of booze; when he left early one morning, I was woken by a bag of clinking empties he was trying to sneak out.

Tony and Ash and I drink away the afternoon, then with Ash's wife Ayde — a receptionist at the town's hospital — we tuck into a tasty dinner in the evening. Turkey with all the trimmings, as Christmas songs play in the background (via YouTube on a laptop). Then, for hours, more beers as we play cards.

At 11 pm, I go to bed — the sofa I'm using as a bed — feeling knackered and coated in sand and dust. I lay there thinking that today is one of the best Christmases I've ever had.

I was a stranger on a bus to Ash, but he took me in and made me welcome. A top bloke. But I'll still be sleeping with one eye open: in the yard, I saw an axe.

ALICE SPRINGS

Alice Springs is the next stop on my multi-day mission northwards to Darwin, to the Timor Sea. Nine hours it took to ride here from Coober Pedy, along that single road, the Stuart Highway, a taut line linking horizons of mammoth emptiness. Nine more hours through burnt red-earth boundless hinterland, just a vast sky and dry scrub and desert; scattered roadhouses but no towns worthy of the name; now and then, a forlorn mailbox, a dirt track to a cattle station out of sight — the largest of them, Anna Creek Station, larger than Israel. I thought: Maybe we could move the Israelis there, solve that whole Middle East thing. The Israelis or the Palestinians, either way works, just flip a coin.

It's surprisingly small, the outback's most famous settlement: a population of only thirty thousand. The biggest town for nearly 1,500 km in any direction, yet just a dry, dusty speck beside the slopes of the MacDonnell Ranges. But this ain't no Aussie Timbuktu, not at all. A grid of streets — Bath Street, Hartley Street, Parsons Street — with a hospital and library and banks, motels and hotels. There's Woolworths and Target; there's McDonald's and Subway. And an airport — for the sane people who don't ride buses for days on end.

More aboriginals than elsewhere I've been, the shadowy, shuffling variety. Not just quietly begging but roaming in groups — shouting, swearing, drinking, pestering, fighting. Hundreds of them, hundreds and hundreds, in old, tatty clothes and with the whiff of those who've spent longer holding a bottle of cheap wine than a bar of soap. I still smile and nod, out of habit. But all that does is invite the inevitable: "Spare a buck, mate?" One with a battered guitar says, "Alright, brother! Where you from? The UK and Oz are like brothers, yeah? So can I have ten dollars for a taxi?" And I see one stood outside the window of McDonald's, knocking it and making hungry gestures; a guy comes out, I think to give some change, but, no; he yells, "Fuck off."

Most who come to Alice Springs come for one reason: That hulking monolith — you know the one. That the two are 400 km apart isn't a care for most, those people having flown here. But an 800 km out-of-the-way roundtrip to see a big rock after you've spent 2,000 km on buses just to get here, well, that needs a second thought. Do I *need* to see it? *Really* need to see it? Might it be a letdown, à la the Opera House? I was burnt by that; its smallness, its shittiness. Reality, travel teaches you, isn't poetry and filters. I umm and err, before deciding that if I do it, I'll hedge my bets with a hike, so even if the rock is shite, at least I'll have been out in "the bush". In a window, I spot an advert for a three-day tour in which you hike, camp, see the rock — that will do. There's a problem, though: "Are you serious?" says the guy in the shop. "You can't wear flip-flops on a hike."

"The aboriginals—," I start to counter before he cuts me off at the start of my aboriginals-don't-wear-trainers argument.

"You're not a bloody aboriginal, though, are you?"

He has me there; I'm not.

I agree to submit to the shoe fascist's demands, but then I find out there's a bunch of other stuff that aboriginals don't need but soft lads like me do: sleeping bag, day bag, torch, insect repellant, towel …

I'm not buying all that stuff for the sake of a three-day trip, so I write off the idea. I'll come back in a few years to do it — and bring a couple of Sherpas with me.

I head to the Alice Springs Reptile Centre — little more than a house with glass boxes in it. I see all sorts of reptiles and snakes, of which Australia has its share and then some. A lethal country is Australia; if you avoid the Great Whites, the saltwater crocodiles might get you; swerve them, and it could be the spiders — the funnel-web or the redback can be deathly. Snakes, though, are its speciality: it has a dozen species that are deadly. The desert death adder: that's well-named; orange-reddish, it camouflages within its surroundings and is a sit-and-wait snake, just chilling in the desert waiting for something to murder with its fangs and venom. I see one of those here and make a note to go back to the tour agency and thank the bloke for saving me from myself. Then there's the taipan snake, the most poisonous on the planet. And here it is, in a glass case, all two metres of it, giving me a look of beady disdain. A bite from him is a one-two of death: Paralysis is served first, with respiratory failure for dessert. That bloke, I'll buy him some chocolates.

A woman working here says she's about to feed some snakes and that I and the few other people here can watch.

"This one's a bloody nasty bastard," she says when we get to one — a carpet python — implying that not all snakes are.

While the snake is curled around the dead mouse she's feeding it on the end of a stick, and the glass front is still off the case, she says we can step closer to take a photo, as when a snake has its prey, it's not interested in anything else. Seconds later, the snake drops the mouse, pauses, then flings itself out the case and onto the floor. I'm first out of the room, with the silver and bronze medals going to two small Chinese women. There's nothing like a bloody nasty bastard of a snake on the loose to make a man forget chivalrous manners.

"More people die from falling off ladders than from snakes," the employee says when the snake is back in its box.

But is that reassuring? I mean, I don't climb ladders; that's an easy thing to avoid. If someone tells me to climb a ladder, I just say, "Climb it yourself." And that's that; they can't make me climb that ladder. But these snakes, and these spiders, all these other things out to get me, they're out there — right outside that door.

The door I exit armed with a longlist of do-not-touch creatures large and small — and some are very small; the redback spider being just 1 cm — to set out to walk to the spring that the town is named after. I take a dirt path that runs beside the Todd River. The river is bone dry, and along its red soil banks are skeletal trees and stunted, gnarled bushes. By the river's dried bed, I see a long-dead kangaroo, its skeleton picked clean. And that's the most alive thing I see. I see no one, see not a thing stirring. Except flies. I see flies, and they see me, come at me, my mouth, nose, ears. I swat them away, but back they come. I'm tormented by them, by their buzzing at every hole. A brute force attack, squadrons of them. I blow from my nose, from my mouth. I slap myself and flap around hopelessly, my hands flailing like I'm attempting an indigenous dance.

Like the Todd River, the spring is dry. Sat by it are a group of kangaroos; I get to within a few metres of them but opt not to go closer, as you never know what the score is with wildlife. The ultimate Aussie Steve Irwin — king of the animals, supposedly — was killed by a fish. So I look from a distance, and think how odd they are, how different to anything that exists in the UK; and I'm not surprised that when word first reached Britain of the weird and wonderful creatures in Australia, some were sceptical ...

"There's a *what* there?"

"A platypus."

"A plate of what?"

"No, platypus. P-l-a-t-y-p-u-s."

"And what's one of those?"

"It's a semi-aquatic mammal. It's furry, with the tail of a beaver and a beak like a duck. Its feet are webbed *and* clawed, and it also has spurs on its feet that are venomous. Oh, and it lays eggs."

"Bollocks, you bloody bullshitter."

"No, really."

"A photo; send me a photo."

"I would, but cameras haven't yet been invented. We won't even have the telegraph for another half a century, which is why this letter correspondence has already taken years. But I'll mail you one so that you can have a look."

And they did just that: sent one back to the UK. But even then, they weren't convinced. The scientists of the times thought it was a hoax, a joke by some comedian taxidermist who'd stitched together odds and sods from all sorts of animals, probably because he had bugger all else to do to pass the time down under, what with there being no bookies or brothels.

Back then, it really did take months for messages to go back and forth between Australia and England. That changed with the arrival of the telegraph, and it's to the tele-graph that Alice Springs owes its existence. It was a repeater station, one of a dozen needed for relaying messages across the length of a country so colossal. The station is here by the spring. Some dude would be sat in it all day, tediously tapping out messages — "Hi Mum. Very hot here. Thinking about building a big bridge. Bye." Then, at the end of the day, he would clock off and go ... well, nowhere, because the telegraph station was all that was here. There was no town; that wouldn't come until years later.

To lay the line for the telegraph was a Herculean endeav-our. The first problem: to find a route across the country. The coast was mapped, but what of the rest of the land? What the heck was out there? They had to find out. And do it on foot. The first explorers had shit to deal with: the heat blazing, and the scarcity of water, and the killer snakes and spiders, and scurvy and sores — that lacerating vegetation pricking their skin, the scratches becoming infected — and the hostile natives with spears. The first were so sure there would be rivers that they took boats. Dragged them they did, for thousands of kilometres, but no water did they find. Others, thirsty, drank their urine to survive. They then drank their horse's piss. Then they died.

John McDouall Stuart was the first to cross Australia, from south to north, through its centre. Into the hellish, baking wilderness, the Scot set off with a few men, a few mules; his map blank mostly, just a white space where he was headed. His first couple of attempts failed; scurvy, in part: his tongue swelled, and his body became a mass of sores. Nine months it took on the third, successful expedition, from Adelaide to the Timor Sea. That was 1861-1862; ten years later, the telegraph line was strung along that route, putting Australia in touch with Britain and beyond. Today's road, the Stuart Highway, is also the same route that Stuart took all those years ago. 2,834 km that road is, and Stuart walked it all. That's 67 marathons.

I start my walk back, back through the murderous and parched and lonely land, thinking of those souls who it has claimed in circumstances inexpressibly tortuous, and thinking what a terrible place to die in, and thinking that I'll go to KFC and get a Zinger burger.

DARWIN

I, at last, reach Darwin on the north coast. Two buses from Alice Springs to Darwin, with Mataranka as a stop-off. Fifteen hours, then seven; long days horizon chasing, monotonously hoovering up the highway through feature-less expanse. The name Stuart is for me now cursed. I'll never again meet a Stuart and not think of that road, those buses. But still, I'm glad I did it, glad I got to see the "real" Oz. The people on Bondi, those on the Gold Coast, those snorkelling the Great Barrier Reef, they think they're in the very heart of Australia, but they have little idea of just how huge and red is this land. The only way to know that is to cross the land by road, ride the long way over the red void, the vast and baking landscape.

The next leg of the trip — to Asia — will need to be by boat (because buses sink). My plan: buy an eyepatch and a copy of *Moby Dick*, and hang around the harbour singing shanties until a ship bound for East Timor or Indonesia — the two closest countries to Darwin — lets me aboard. But the receptionist at the hostel says I'd be better off shaving and wearing a clean shirt, then going to the Darwin Sailing Club — so I do that instead.

I ask the barman there about boats going to Asia.

He says, "Not at this time of year. You've timed it wrong. Darwin has a tropical climate: it's sunny for most of the year, but now it's the start of the stormy season. Come back in June; loads of yachts go to Asia at that time."

On the way back to the hostel, I chat to Terry: a sixty-something-year-old with a flannel on his head, stood drinking beer beside a camper van. He tells me: "Dinah Beach Cruising Yacht Association is your best shot. That's where the lower-class yachties hang out. I used to be a regular there, but they barred me for getting pissed and starting fights."

A thirty-minute stroll later, shadeless kilometres on a sultry day, I sweatily arrive at the Dinah Beach Cruising Yacht Association. The bargirl points to a couple of bearded sailor-types at a table in the corner and says that they're the ones to ask. I go over to them.

Me: "Do you know anyone who's sailing to Asia soon?"

Sailor One: "Ha! Do you hear that?! The pom wants to go to Asia!"

Sailor Two: "You'd be unlucky if you found someone to take you. They'd be taking you to your death. It's the cyclone season."

Me: "Cyclones? In Darwin?"

Sailor Two: "Yeah, don't you know about Cyclone Tracy? Christmas Eve '74, it damn near blew away the place. Winds over a hundred miles an hour. Billions of bucks of damage it caused. People died."

Sailor One: "Even if you avoid one of those, the rough seas at this time of year can flip over a boat easy."

Sailor Two: "We know everyone here, and they'll all say no, but if you've got a death wish, you could try your luck down the road at Tipperary Waters Marina."

At Tipperary Waters Marina, yachts are moored, but its bars and shops are closed. The noticeboard is bare but for a few adverts offering boats for sale. If I call my bank to ask for £15,000 to buy a boat so that I can sail to Asia, they'll tell me to sod off — and also ask me when I'm paying back what I already owe them. I'm about to leave when I spot a man exit a yacht to go to his car. He tells me: "You won't find anyone to take you. Not going to happen. No chance. No way. You can buy a rubber dinghy and have a go yourself. Or you can fly: it's only £100 to fly to Bali."

That ends my plan to sail to Asia.

If I wait for months for the weather to improve, it will blow a huge hole in my tinpot budget. The girl at the hostel reception mentioned that they take on volunteers — changing bed sheets, cleaning toilets and floors, etc. in exchange for a free bed and food — but fuck that for a week, never mind for months. And to wait will mean I'll have to do the rest of the journey out of season. I'd then be travelling through Asia in the rainy season and getting to Europe as the winter kicks in — not an option for a bloke in flip-flops.

But I won't fly. It's all or nothing, this journey. No: "I travelled from Australia to Europe without flying ... well, except for that one flight I took from Australia to Bali." No, take one flight, and the game is lost.

In the evening, I go to Mindil Beach. The sun lowers, sinks into the sea, and the sky is a burst of colours — barred shades of pink and indigo, bright orange streaks. I stare at the serene sweep of bay and think about East Timor; it's right across this sea, just 600 km from this spot. Surely there's a way?

I'd probably not quite make the swim, what with my backpack weighing me down. And there's a thing or two in that sea, a thing or two that is cruelly savage in that peculiarly Australian manner. Maybe no sea on earth is as lethal as this one here, the one I have to cross. Sharks and stingrays and saltwater crocodiles and blue-ringed octopuses — that last one, only the size of a golf ball, but whose caress kills within half an hour. Oh, and box jellyfish, the deadliest creature in all the seas. *One* could decimate a wedding — up to sixty people. Its venomous, thread-like tentacles, up to three metres in length, sting the shit out of you. Delirium. Paralysis. Cardiac arrest. And the bag of death doesn't even give you a fair chance to avoid it: it's almost transparent in the water. A nasty fucker, no doubt, and this very sea is full of them; signs along the beach say so, warn "DANGER: Box Jellyfish: Do Not Enter The Water."

That's what's in the sea, but there's also just the sea: It swallowed an Australian Prime Minister, Harold Holt. He went in for a swim and never came back. Poof — gone forever, vanished. His body never found. A conspiracy theory says a Chinese submarine picked him up, part of some elaborate scheme for him to defect to China. But those conspiracy theorist blokes, well, you know what they're like. The earth is flat, is it? Ok, mate. Have you seen much of it? No, never been outside of Kentucky? Thought so. And we're ruled by shape-shifting reptilian aliens, are we? Any chance of a photo? Oh, you left your camera at home that day.

So swim, no. But a raft of some sort? That's how the first aboriginals arrived here. So it's thought, anyway. They came here from somewhere — that the nerds agree on — because Australia has no apes from which humans could descend. And they didn't walk: Australia has been an island the whole time man has been on the earth. So by sea then. But there's a flaw in that idea: That was at a time when no one else on earth was advanced enough to do such a thing as build boats that could cross the sea — and wouldn't be smart enough to do so for thousands of years. And those people would have had no idea Australia even existed. To believe that theory, that they came by sea, you must accept that they had boats from thousands of years ahead of their time and set off into the big blue sea on the off chance that they'd find land and did so in numbers enough to start a colony. So I'm with the conspiracy theorists on that one: Aliens.

Darwin is in the tropics, closer to Jakarta than Adelaide, on the same latitude as Mozambique and Bolivia, but you'd never guess that from the look of it. It's dull and tired and could be Dundee. The weather, however, there's no mistaking that for the UK. At thirty-six degrees, yesterday was the highest January temperature in Darwin since records began. Washing I hung out was dry in a few hours.

This morning, though, it's raining non-stop, and there's a brooding menace in the sombre sky. The news issued a warning: a cyclone currently off the north coast of Australia may hit Darwin tonight or tomorrow. So I deflate the rubber dinghy I bought — that I spent all of yesterday blowing up — and return it to the shop.

While out, an idea occurs: Travel to Asia by cruise ship;

not from Darwin, but from somewhere in the south, out of reach of cyclones. Down there, it's still warm and dry. Too warm, in fact, and too dry. Bushfires are roaring — flames fifty metres high — and Adelaide just had their fourth hottest day on record: forty-five degrees.

A woman at a travel agency on the high street asks how she can help.

I tell her, "I'd like to book a cruise, please."

"Where to and when?"

"Anywhere in Australia to anywhere in Asia, leaving anytime in the next month."

She looks at me like I'm an idiot, but after I explain about the trip and promise that she'll get to play herself in the movie of the book, she does her best to help. She finds a Brisbane to Shanghai cruise for £900 that departs next week. But it's fully booked. Most people, she says, book cruises six-to-twelve months in advance, not the week before. She finds only one that still has tickets available: Sydney to Southampton. To take one boat from Australia to Europe would simplify the journey, but it's expensive: £9,500. I ask for an £8,500 discount. She says no.

The only option left is to travel from Australia to Asia on a cargo ship. I've heard this is possible, but I've never met anyone who's done it. It's one of those a-friend-of-a-friend's-brother-in-law's-sister's-friend-knows-someone-who-might-have-done-it-a-few-years-ago things. I Google "cargo shipping companies in Australia" and find a dozen. None of their websites mentions anything about transporting passengers, but I email all of them anyway.

That done, and hoping a good deed will earn me some good luck, I go to the Red Cross Blood Donor Centre. A nurse there asks if I lived in the UK between 1980 and 1996.

I tell her, "Yes, for most of that time, from when I was born in 1983 until after 1996."

"We don't accept blood from anyone who spent more than six months in the UK between those dates due to the risk of mad cow disease."

I offer her my other products, but she declines those as well, so I put them back in the Tupperware and leave.

Replies rolled in from the shipping companies; they all said they don't transport passengers. But one reply had advice in addition to the knock-back: the guy advised searching for "freighter travel". I did so and found a company that specialises in booking people onto cargo ships. I contacted them and bought a ticket to travel from Adelaide to Singapore. Good news but not ideal: it was pricey (£1,200), and Adelaide is back where I've come from — where I've travelled fifty-plus hours on buses to come from. A wise man would have researched the weather in Darwin before coming, realised sailing wasn't viable, and bought a ticket for a cargo ship that departed from Sydney. I'm an idiot, though, not a wise man.

Screw taking buses back the exact route I came up on. I can't face that road again, those 2,834 km of tarmac. I'll take the train instead; it's the same route, that vast, bleak expanse of monotonous nothingness, but on a train, it might at least feel a little different.

So now I'm stood in a drenching downpour under a slate-grey sky, at the train pick-up point in the town centre, waiting with other passengers to be driven to the station. The remnants of last night's storm, this is: all night, the wind howled, and lightning streaked; the hostel creaked, its windows rattled. A rep from the company comes — a uni-student-type in an ill-fitting uniform — to tell us the train is delayed because three hundred metres of track have flooded, the embankments possibly washed away. He says he'll update us in an hour. As we're waiting, a guy walks past and asks what we're doing; he laughs about the train then points at a bloke in a wheelchair: "He'll be alright, though." — like wheeling himself a few thousand kilometres to Adelaide is an option.

The update comes: Train cancelled; there won't be another one for two weeks.

I check back into the hostel — and am laughed at by a roommate who said last night that it would be funny if the track blew away — and revise my plan. The plan I come up with, the only choice available: bloody buses. But I speak with the shipping company and arrange to board the ship at Fremantle instead of Adelaide. Fremantle is in the south-west, near Perth. It's 4,000 km from Darwin, whereas Adelaide is only 3,000 km, but it means I won't have to take that same damn road I did on the way up here. It's just two buses. The first, twenty-four hours. The second, thirty-fuck-ing-six. I could fly anywhere in the world in less time.

BROOME TO PERTH

This YHA hostel in Broome is dreadful. Blue lino floor in the dorm; tatty, brown curtains; a four-drawer cabinet with one drawer missing. It's boiling because there's a slot to put coins into to pay for the air-con, and, of course, nobody wants to be the one to pay up; and the internet is slow as heck — 10-20 seconds to load a page. It's very laddie; lots of bulky, tattooed blokes who are working, not travelling. Some have been at the hostel for months. There's Joe, a Scouse plumber, working on tourist visas. A couple of builders: one Irish, one Northern Irish — who both lay claim to their brand of Irish being the hardest workers. A French fella painting a school (£12 an hour, cash in hand) — before he worked at a harbour, unloading prawn boats. And a guy who spent a month sorting potatoes into piles: "I had to put the good potatoes, the big, good quality ones, into one pile, and the small or damaged potatoes into a second pile. Good potato, bad potato, good potato, bad potato, for twelve hours a day."

Another bloke here, Luke, is like a yo-yo, in and out of rooms. He's a recovering alcoholic. He says he worked as a bouncer in Darwin but now runs a Facebook page selling novelty ID cards. A torrent of chatter, he goes on a tangent about 9/11 conspiracy theories, says this week he'll make a three-hour video based on four years of research. His edgy pal — a German — is the same, in recovery from something; he rants to me about FEMA camps — a conspiracy theory about the US government planning to impose martial law to imprison citizens. When I ask why they'd do that, he goes on about "The New World Order". This sets Luke off at length about shadowy organisations running the world and country leaders being no more than puppets. The German says that they're Jews. Luke agrees. Luke has been at the hostel for months but is now out of money, so he's going to stay with his gran. "That thousand bucks I spent on New Years Day, I regret that now. It was fun, those five hours with a couple of Chinese hookers, but I could really do with that cash."

To pass some time until the bus goes, I walk to Town Beach. I stand on the grassy verge that leads down to the red sand. A miserable greyness again in the sky. A ragtag bunch of pissed locals come over, all aboriginals. The women have their hands all over me, and tell me who's single. There's a moody bloke with a bagged bottle in his hand; scabs on his face, teeth missing. "Shake him down," says one of the girls to the bloke. Me and the guy eye each other, him weighing me up. I look at his bony shell, his rumpled clothing. I'd beat his ass. He laughs and says not to worry, then the girl slaps him in the face and tells him to fuck off. He slaps her back. He tells me if I go to Cable Beach, I might see a camel; then asks me for a dollar, like his advice was worth that much. He rambles at me for ten minutes until a scene at the off-licence over the road catches his interest: another aboriginal being bundled into a police truck. Spooked by that, the bloke with me legs it.

Back at the hostel, I chill in the "lounge" — a corrugated rusty roof; bean bags strewn around — and put on a DVD of *Ferris Bueller's Day Off* to pass some more time. Then I take a long shower and brush my teeth, put on my cleanest clothes. I look and feel fresh, but how long will that last? About six hours, I reckon.

The bus pick-up point is Broome Visitor Centre. The other passengers are predominantly aboriginals, and half look pissed. A war vet — his medals on show — in a wheelchair has been drinking with them. I thought I'd gotten used to bus travel, but I have that slightly dreading feeling again. Broome to Perth — thirty-six hours — is 50% longer than the one I did a couple of days ago, and that was already far and away my longest journey. It was empty, mostly, between Darwin and Broome. Even greater stretches of emptiness to come.

Two drivers: Joe, fifty-plus, and Steve, his young apprentice. Joe is Yoda-like; Steve more Jabba than Skywalker. Both wear schoolboy-style uniforms: dark-blue shirts with too-short light-blue shorts; white socks pulled up nearly to the knee. Joe says the bus's clutch is broken, which explains why the bus jumped into the car park. *Jumped!* It bounced in like a clown-mobile. I don't drive, have never owned a vehicle, but I know that the clutch, while not as important as, say, the wheels, is pretty important. He says starting and stopping will be bumpy, so to hang on tight. "We're not really sure what it's going to do; it's sort of unpredictable. We're not happy about driving like this, but the man who pays the bills ..." He's properly stressed, smokes three fags in half an hour.

A broken clutch, no seatbelts, pissed passengers, and a crying baby: not a good start.

At 8 pm, we leave. The sky is black against the window. Lightning streaks across the sky. The lights on the bus are dim, and the air is cold. A little snoring, a whiff from the toilet. *Cable Guy* plays on the bus TVs, then *The Bourne Legacy*, but I can't hear half the words despite the volume being loud — and half the words is way worse than none. It's not great being on this bus, not great at all, but where would I rather be? Slumped on a comfy sofa, flicking through channels, frittering hours away? In a pub, pissed on Carling? No, I've been there, done that. I'd rather be right here, doing what I'm doing: on a bus in the boonies, riding to the coast, to a cargo ship — a ship bound for Singapore. I made a choice: Be home or elsewhere, and this bus — shit as it is — is my elsewhere right now.

The night hours pass slow — 1 am, 2 am, 3 am ... — sleep coming and going. I half-think, half-dream, travel the outback of my mind. Memories strobe past, and I recall much I thought I'd forgotten: That time I ... That other time, with the ... And that girl, the one with the sexy knees — I wonder what she's up to now ... Oh, and Dave, he still owes me £20 from that night at The Masons ...

I'm jerked to startled wakefulness when we stop at Karratha at 6 am, with the sky slowly lightening. Some kids laugh at us bounce into the station; hilarious, I'm sure, to anyone not on the bus. Now out of the north, away from the storms, the morning is beautiful, and on we go, under a vast blue sky, a near-full moon still bright.

At 8.50 am, we pick up a Taiwanese woman at a bus stop miles from anywhere — outback to the horizon. She's been stood under a metal shelter, waiting; there's the shelter and two picnic tables and sod all else. If the bus didn't come, she'd have been screwed. And she was worried, she tells me: no phone signal and the bus was late. I tell her I've come from Broome and that I thought Broome YHA was skanky. She says she stayed there a couple of years ago, says a guy on the bottom bunk was watching porn and wanking. I say the stains are probably still on the sheets.

I've spoken to only one other on the bus, back at a stop last night: an old dude keen to tell me his woes. His wife ran off with another woman; he hasn't seen his four kids for ten years.

Over a thousand kilometres already. Obviously, the distance is a killer, but it's not just the kilometres that wear you down; it's the emptiness, the epic, tedious backdrop. No landmarks, nothing to tick off. All the same. A hundred kilometres in Australia isn't the same as a hundred in Britain. Drive that distance in England, say from Leeds to Nottingham, and you'll see all sorts of towns on the way, will see Sheffield and Barnsley and Rotherham, will see signposts in between, regular and reassuring, little milestones to spur you on. Not places you'd want to go, of course, Sheffield or Barnsley or Rotherham, but at least they're there, there with their Greggs and Wetherspoons.

Every hour or three, a forlorn roadhouse or a dirt track off to an unseen something — a mine, maybe, or a cattle station. A refinery, at one point, a flame from its top. Sometimes a prefab house, or a digger, a group of workmen. I see five cows stood around a large termite mound; not in a field, just bare desert, no shade at all. And a rusted fridge by the side of the road: "05/09 — Remove to tip" sprayed in white on it. Otherwise, nothing but red earth, scrubby vegetation. It just goes on and on and on, that red, on and on, and also the time too. Tick-tock, tick-tock, but the clock feels as though it's stopped. Minutes lengthen; elongated are the hours. I doze and wake and look to see in hope — hope for a change, anything — but just more red, on and on and on; the lonely highway through the middle of it; the road that rolls on and on. No one who says, "It's a small world, eh?" has ever taken buses across Australia.

No phone, no wifi; so no check, check, check — news and emails, Facebook and football scores ... And that's good, in a way; it's a disease, that checking repetitiously. So I listen to a Sven Vath Essential Mix, also Charles Dickens's *Our Mutual Friend* audiobook. I get lost in reverie for a while, and at times meditate — badly. I call the roll of all I've ever known who are now dead, and I resurrect them in my mind. And I list the register of my Year 4 class: Amy Beech, Adam Capewell, Jordan Cadbury, Claire Fisher ... And I recall who played for Aston Villa in the 1994 Coca-Cola Cup Final: Mark Bosnich, Earl Barrett and Steve Staunton, Shaun Teale and Paul McGrath and Andy Townsend, Dalian Atkinson and Tony Daley ...

But there's just too much time to fill, and excruciating monotony sinks in that eats at my soul.

Be patient, I tell myself. A day and a half on a bus is a long time — and it feels like it now — but in a lifetime, even in a month, it's nothing. Brutal days end, and the pain passes; what remains is the satisfaction of accomplishment. And, I tell myself, compared to a real job — working on a supermarket checkout, shuffling numbers around a spreadsheet at an insurance company, being a night porter at a hotel (all three of which I've done) — travelling is nothing hard. I don't have to do a thing but wait.

And isn't all life just waiting anyway?

Waiting in queues, in traffic jams. Waiting for 5 pm, for the weekend, for your vacation. Waiting for Christmas to come, then for winter to end. For the flowers of spring, for the red, falling leaves of autumn. Waiting for the one. Waiting for the kids to leave home, then waiting for them to come and visit once or twice a year. Then, at last, old and sick and tired, waiting for the end, for the final sleep.

So waiting for this bus to go from here to there, well, so what? That other waiting is harder, longer. Whereas to this waiting, there is nothing complicated. I just have to sit, sit and wait, no one asking anything of me, no one telling me what to do.

So I sit and stare out the window, and watch the empty world slowly go by, and think about the irony of travelling: that you need to be able to sit still.

At Exmouth, just past midday, I see the Indian Ocean, a glorious and inviting blue, and the road runs by it for a while, a break from that damn red. Two emus cross the road as we set off again after Exmouth. I'm sure there's a joke in there somewhere — "Why did the emus cross the road?" — and I've the time to waste to think of one, but I can't. A couple of hours pass, and we stop at Coral Bay: A caravan park, holidaying families. I pick up hummus and a couple of bread rolls, for a man can't live on nuts and Kit-Kats alone, but I soon regret the choice: I feel bloated, shouldn't have eaten so much. It sits like a stone in my stomach.

At 5.55 pm, we arrive in Carnarvon for a dinner stop for an hour. A stop greatly welcome, both for time to walk and time to shit. I get to the shopping centre three minutes before it closes, which is a lucky break as it's never great to announce your arrival at a place by taking a dump in the park. I breathe the breeze at the harbour, wash my feet and face in the sea. I take off my shirt and lie on some grass by a beach. An ideal break, this is; I couldn't have asked for more.

Twenty newbies board. To them, I must look like a hobo, and they're not far wrong. I'm the last one left on the bus from those who started in Broome. So, I win. Though what exactly I've won, I'm not sure. No one but the drivers know my pain. I'm at least ten hours up on everyone else.

My bag being small enough to be on board with me, rather than in the hold, means I can change into a jumper — it gets chilly at night — and take a finger of toothpaste. Then it's bedtime, trying again to sleep in the seat, the seat I've sweated and farted on today, the seat I went to sleep in last night and this morning woke up in. I kip on and off, see the dark streets of Geraldton at 1.30 am and, at 4.55 am, we pull over at some random place and all move onto a new bus — after thirty-three hours with that fucking broken clutch. I even beat the bus itself.

I watched the sunset on my right last night; now I watch

it rise to the left, as Perth comes on along Indian Ocean Drive, and the land has life again: Sheep in meadowy landscapes. Trees — big, green trees! Enough to at times be called forests. I'm back in the Shire, it seems, after a stint in Mordor.

We drive past a train station, Edgewater; twenty suited people outside it, grim at the thought of the office. A traffic jam, the Monday morning rush, then, "Welcome to Perth," says Joe, as we pull into Wellington Street Station at 7.05 am.

Thirty-five hours and five minutes: I've completed buses.

INDIAN OCEAN

Perth was clean, modern, welcoming. No particular distinction, but a fine enough place to live. I'd choose there over Sydney or Melbourne, were it not so stranded. It's as close to Singapore as it is to Sydney, though not actually close to either: 4,000 km to one or the other. The nearest city to it is Adelaide, just 2,500 km of red desert emptiness in between — a long way to go for a weekend break to see the world's biggest rocking horse.

Fremantle is a 25-minute train ride from Perth. At the entrance to its North Quay Harbour, a queue of trucks wait. I walk past them, past the eyes of the drivers looking down at the odd fella in flip-flops. I sit in the security gatehouse, waiting for them to check my story — my story of riding a freighter to Singapore. I get the all-clear, and a security guard drives me to one of the ships, drives me past giant cranes, past thousands of containers, past men in yellow jackets buzzing around. I climb steep metal stairs onto the deck, from where a Filipino bloke — Bernardo — takes me to a seven-floor structure towards the back of the ship that spans almost its width; in it are offices, bedrooms, dining rooms. My room is one of a few kept spare for journeys that require extra crew. It has a lounge, bedroom, and bathroom, and is furnished like a suite at a 3-star hotel. A TV, a DVD player, and a HiFi system (with tape deck). And towels: *Three! Decadence!* Everything is strapped in place, including an artificial potted plant in the corner — the straps to stop things falling in rough seas. Other signs that life at sea might not be smooth: A yellow hard hat and life jacket hang on wall hooks, and on a table is a large black holdall, a white label stitched onto it: "Solas smart suit type 2a. An insulated immersion suit / anti-exposure suit. Made in Scunthorpe."

Bernardo gives me an information booklet, tells me to wait in my room, then leaves. The booklet looks like it was created in the mid-nineties when clipart was cutting edge and anyone with Microsoft Publisher was a graphic designer. Images used include bananas, dancers, flowers — none have any relevance to the text. I learn that the ship is called MSC Uganda (but is German, not Ugandan). It's 294 metres long; it can hold 4,545 shipping containers. Those stats make it sound like a beast, yet it's one of the smallest ships here.

I wait, watch the cranes, snooze for a while, and slowly hours pass. The TV won't pick up a signal, and there's no wifi — the only internet access is via a computer in the captain's office. I'd like a walk, see what's what on the ship, but Bernardo said to stay put, and I don't want to piss off the crew at least until we've set sail and it's too late for them to kick me off. Noon passes, and still I wait. So much of travel is waiting, watching the clock: tick-tock, tick-tock, tick-tock …

After six hours idle in my room, I get a call on the in-room phone and am told to go to an office to meet the captain: a German in his late-fifties named Waldemar Murawski. I like that name; it's strong-sounding, seaworthy. I wouldn't be happy with a captain called Malcolm Shuffle-bottom. I'd trust Malcolm Shufflebottom to drive a bus, but not a cargo ship. "Welcome aboard, Herr Walters," he says as he crushes my fingers with his handshake. He tells me I'm free to go wherever I want on the ship. "You must be careful, though," he adds. "There are many ways you can injure yourself. You can fall over things; things can fall on you. And if you fall into the sea, it's a major problem — for us, and for you, but more for you." Then he gives me an indemnity form to sign; it says that I give up my rights to make any claims against the shipping company, even if they've been negli-gent. I ask if I can help out, put in a shift with a spanner, but he says no, I'm not allowed to legally; it would void their insurance if I screw up. For the best, really, as I'm useless with a spanner, or indeed with anything practical. If I can't copy-paste something, and if there's not a delete button, it's better to leave it to someone else.

Back to my room, again waiting; then sirens sound: abandon ship — a drill. As instructed in the information booklet, I grab the life jacket and hard hat and head to the port-side lifeboat. I'm first there and feel smug to be. Ten minutes later, I feel less smug: a spectacled mechanic comes to get me to take me to the other side of the ship. I've been stood at the starboard-side lifeboat. Not my only faux-pas: I've come in a t-shirt and flip-flops, like I'm off to the beach. "You must wear a jumper," I'm told — told off, in fact, by the second-in-command, the chief officer. "It's cold at sea, *ja*?"

"*Ja*," I agree, speaking German as well as I can.

"And flip-flops, no. Trainers, you must wear trainers when you are out on deck. It's dangerous at sea, *ja*?"

"*Ja*. But, err, I don't have any."

He frowns and shakes his head, gives me the look one gives a child who's eating crayons. "Then you will have to borrow trainers, *ja*?"

All the crew are here. The officers, engineers, and mechanics are German (except for Filipino Bernardo); the deckhands — those that do the hard, dirty work — are Kiribatian. I've never before heard of Kiribati, and it sounds as made up as Narnia. I'm told it's an island nation in the middle of the Pacific Ocean, and as there's no wifi, I'll have to take their word for it.

A few crew get in the lifeboat, lower it down to the water, and circle around for a while. As that's happening, I speak to the spectacled mechanic — a veteran; forty-six years on ships. He says 24/7 he's responsible for fixing anything and everything — big and small, from the engine to the toilets. He works for 3-to-4 months, then gets a month off to go home. He says this ship has gone from Europe to the US to South America to Africa to Australia, and after Singapore will go to the Middle East.

I say, "Must be fun to get to see all those places."

"But all we get to see are the docks. We have to work the

whole time the ship is at a port. We don't get time off to look around, go sightseeing or shopping or drinking."

I ask about pirates. "Around Africa — Somalia and Yemen — you're at risk?"

"We don't worry about pirates because of the speed of our ship."

"But they must have ships that are fast; surely speedboats?"

"Yes, they have fast boats — actually faster than ours — but if the ship they're trying to board is moving quickly, it's difficult for them to get their ropes or ladders attached. And look how big our ship is; it's not easy to climb up here, especially if the captain keeps changing direction and speed."

"Guns, though; you have some? A few grenades?"

"No, we have none."

I guess they could improvise if they had to: use potatoes from the kitchen. While not as effective as a grenade, a well-aimed potato can cause a bruise.

Night falls, and we're still at port. Until, at 11 pm, a couple of tugboats latch on to the ship and pull us away from the dock. Then the ship's engine kicks in. I walk out onto the deck. A strong smell of oil in the air. With one hand, I hold onto a railing; with the other, I cling to my hard hat — it's so windy that it's at risk of blowing off. After fifteen minutes, we pass the lighthouse that marks the end of the harbour, and we're out at sea and soon rolling and pitching.

Back in my room, the wardrobe flies open, and my shower gel falls off its stand, and the curtains slide from side to side. As I lay in bed, I feel nauseous. The room spins like it does at the end of a night of too much boozing. The captain said many people get seasick during their first time at sea and that it can last for days. As I lay awake, awake and sick, I recap, again and again, what to do if we have to abandon the ship: grab the hard hat, the life jacket, a jumper; go down to A-Deck, turn right and go out the door at the end of the corridor, then go up one flight of stairs. I think: I could save some seconds if I sleep fully clothed. So I get out of bed and put them on, and while I'm up, put on the lifejacket and hard hat as well — a few more saved seconds. Then I move from the bed to the sofa; nearer to the door —

more seconds saved — and to lay against the swaying: instead of rolling side to side, my head and feet go up and down. It helps a little, but the creaks, cracks, and whirrs — that come from above and below, left and right — keep me awake, and I know I'm a prisoner to a sleepless night that will inch into dawn.

———

Swells in the sea — big ones — and still the ship rolls from side to side, but after a pep talk in the mirror — "Come on; you're a big boy, a big, big boy ..." — I don my hard hat and borrowed trainers and brave the deck. The ship's sides are too high for water to splash the deck, but the breaking waves make mist-like the air. The engine thrums, and I feel its might from below, and I hear the contents of containers sliding about. The barriers that border the ship's outer edge are only half a metre high, and the walkway is no more than a metre wide. I grip the rail — dirt and salt coat my hands — and nudge myself along at a pace only slightly quicker than stationary. "... a big boy ..." I remind myself, "... a big, big boy ..." for the ten minutes it takes me to reach the bow, where is an anchor — its chain as thick as my waist. After I sing *My Heart Will Go On*, I'm eager to return to my room, as I really could die out here: a big swell, a tumble over the side. The sea is unforgiving, merciless. In the outback, it at least takes days to die; in the sea, you could be doomed in minutes. It's claimed many more souls than the earth's deserts or mountains. To be lost and never found is probable. Which would be a bonus for my Dad — after the initial tears: "Well, he was the middle child, but we'll still miss him." — as he told me more than once before I left to make sure I have good travel insurance that covers shipping my body back, as it can cost up to £10,000. I ignored that and got cheap travel insurance (because it was cheap).

Back to my room to free my feet in flip-flops, then I head up to the "bridge" — the ship's cockpit. In it is a steering wheel thingy (not the official nautical name), a large control panel with hundreds of buttons and dials, and three monitors — two display radars and one a map. The map is super detailed; it shows not only where land is but sea depths and danger points. I see that we've detoured around an area marked "Explosives Dumping Ground". Bernardo is currently controlling the ship. He says he does two four-hour shifts here a day. If it's daytime, it's a one-man job, but they have two up here at night as there's a risk that a man alone may nod off. It's a risk because there's not all that much to do. He tells me: "It runs on autopilot except when near land or when passing through a congested shipping lane."

"Punch in the coordinates, then chill?"

He laughs. "Not exactly. We still need to watch out for other ships. And keep an eye on the speed — reduce it if there are large waves to prevent containers falling off or damage to the ship."

"How often does that happen? Containers falling off?"

"It's rare, but it does happen. At my previous company, we lost three tiers during a severe storm."

I leave Bernardo to go down for lunch in the officers' mess-room, where I eat all my meals. A waiter serves us food; he calls everyone "sir" — he calls me it too. He looks a bit shabby, with DIY turn-ups on his black trousers (each stitch large and white), but still, always good to be a "sir". Proper food, a full-time chef — a nice change from Australia, where for two months I survived on tins of beans and canned fruit, bags of nuts and Kit-Kats. Spaghetti today. Yesterday, we had Chicken curry; another day, mashed potato and chicken steak; beef and boiled potatoes, that we had too, as well as chilli con carne. We sit at four tables of four, with everyone in the same seat for each meal. Sit in near silence; barely a sound other than cutlery, hardly a murmur. They must run out of things to say after months of sitting next to each other for three meals a day — especially when they have no news or weekends to discuss. There are only so many times you can debate the best size and colour of shipping container before the topic gets dull.

"Herr Ernst, did you see the game last night?"

"No, Ulrich, I didn't. We're on a ship; there's no TV. I never see the game. You never see the game. No one on this ship ever sees the game."

"Ah, right, of course. So what did you do last night?"

"Nothing. I was with you. We both did nothing. We sat and talked about how we did nothing the night before. We had this same exact conversation — like we do every night."

"That's not true; not *every* night. There was that one night we were so bored that we—"

"We must never ever talk of that night. Never."

Later, land ahoy! We pass palmy coasts, tropical islands covered in jungle. Asia: to be precise, Indonesia. To the left, the island of Sumatra; to the right, Java. This the Sunda Strait that links the Indian Ocean to the Java Sea. And here the sea is calm, and its colour changed: from a dark blue to a soft blue-green.

I watch the scene from F-Deck (the top floor of the ship), sat on a deckchair, the sun on my face, the wind in my hair, and think: This is a moment, the sort of moment to travel for. I think too that probably these are the best days of my life, the days of this trip — days past, days to come. I know that now and don't need longing hindsight. Here, now: The dream being lived.

"I'm jealous," some say. "I wish I could do that." And I tell them they can. Then they say, "I will, but next year, or the year after. Before I'm forty, 100%. Fifty at the latest." But I know they won't.

Others say, "Mark, shouldn't you settle down? Get married? A house?" I hear that more and more since I turned thirty a year ago. Asked by boring bastards, that settling-down question often is; those chained to their town, their norm, to a career, getting a mortgage; those bouncing between an office and a sofa, saving, boozing, and shagging, stockpiling cushions and shoes. The "done thing" done, day after day. Shitty drudgery, fussing at the margins, suspended in a vegetative stupor; counting the empty hours down to 5 pm, to casual Fridays, to a weekend of prosecco and Netflix. Lives of quiet desperation; idly complaining, discontented. Quietly stagnating while simultaneously frantically posting Facebook photos to prove the opposite.

I've opted out of that life, opted into this one — a life that's uncertain, but a life that's chosen, not just the done-thing-default. As soon as real-life came, as soon as I sensed that suffocating routine, I set off for a more breathable atmosphere. I went to Thailand, went to Korea, went beyond. I swam away from the mainstream, and I'm still at it — doggy-paddling my way to ... well, let's see where. Maybe I can't do this forever — on the seas, on open roads, without obligations nor responsibilities, no compromises nor constraints — but I can do it for now, press the pause button for reality until I'm forty at least. The way I see it, most people live until they're about eighty, and those years should be split between being settled and being unsettled. Eighty divided by two equals forty years of each. So it mathematically makes sense not to settle until you're forty. You can't argue with maths. To think you'll work hard when you're young, then go wild when you're retired, is bollocks. By the time people retire, they're mostly worn out; their vigour and enthusiasm wilted at best, died at worst.

Now I have my youth, my health, and diamonds they both are. I won't waste them on a hunt for riches and respectability — that's for sure. Freedom: that's what those diamonds will be spent on. Freedom to go here, to go there, to go anywhere; to wake up when I want to wake up, to eat a bowl of Coco-Pops at three in the afternoon; to quench my fancies, to explore the cracks of the world, to seek for the weird and wonderful, for novelty and for awe. Oh yes — sweet, glorious freedom.

And so on this bench, this bench on the MSC Uganda, the MSC Uganda cruising to Singapore, I'm glad I've left all that — the prison of routine, the humdrum ordinariness — left it for days clothed in uncertainty, to go mining for the extraordinary, digging deep; one day finding treasure, the next a dead body or a turd. And I will have my reward, so long as all I want are laughs and stories to tell.

Back to F-Deck at 6 pm for a barbecue. Most of the crew are here; the Kiribatians as well, but they keep to themselves, don't mix with the Germans. We eat steaks and sausages, baked potatoes, garlic bread, salad, beans. And drink beers, lots of beers — bought from the ship's shop, which opens for an hour a day. The shop sells beers (£9 for a crate of twenty-four Warsteiner bottles) and cigarettes (£7 for a 200-carton), as well as Ritter Sport chocolate and other foodstuffs from Germany — little tastes of home to see them through the long months away.

As we eat and drink, I ask the captain what he does with his free time on the ship.

He says, "I have no free time. I get email after email to deal with. It didn't use to be like this. Ten years ago, I'd get one lot of papers when I left a port, and that would be it until the next port when I'd get more. Now, because of these auto-pilot ships, they think I should deal with the stuff they used to do in their offices. When I was a child, my dream was to be a captain, but I never dreamed it would be like this: doing admin all day long. I don't want to work like this, but what can I do? It's the way the job is now. Not like when I started, when to be a captain you really had to know how to sail a ship, and you'd be at the bridge all day, sailing — *really* sailing. These days, the younger ones don't know much, don't know how to sail. If you took their tools away, they wouldn't know what to do. But they're good with computers, with spreadsheets, and that's what the shipping companies look for now. And they also want yes-men, guys who do what they're told. The reason for the delay at Fremantle was that I wanted more fuel before we departed, but head office said we had enough. There was only 250 tons of fuel put by for us, even though I told them a month ago that we need 350. I told them that to leave without 350 isn't safe. We argued, and, at last, they gave in, and I got the 100 extra. Who made that decision to say we need only 250 tons? Someone in an office who's never sailed these ships. Whereas I've sailed for decades, yet I still have to argue about stuff like that."

The night ends up with me and a couple of Germans listening to techno, rat-arsed on Warsteiner. Not a bad birthday, one that ends like that: drunk on a cargo ship in the Java Sea.

A week I've been on the ship. We may reach Singapore today, but I don't know. There are only so many times you can ask, "Are we nearly there yet?" — and I feel I've already exceeded that limit.

I've by now stopped looking out my windows: there's nothing to see but sea. The seven DVDs here I've watched: *The Matrix*, *The Matrix Reloaded*, *Enemy At The Gates*, and a few others. One day, I went to the gym, pool, and sauna. Once was enough. The sauna is the size of a fat man's coffin; the pool is a small metal box filled with seawater; the gym has only three pieces of antiquated weightlifting equipment. To properly exercise, the only option is to run in circles — small circles because there's no space to run in large ones. The crew go months at a time without any decent exercise, which (along with the stodgy food) explains the chunky bellies. They get paid well and aren't stressed or overworked — just eight hours a day they do — but the boredom must take its toll. Every day the same, just ticking them off until they can go home. It's a cooped-up existence and one I'd struggle with. For me, to be on board is a novelty, but a week is plenty to play at being a sailor. I'll be glad to be back on terra firma, where I can run in circles as large as I like.

At 1.30 am, an alarm sounds, then the phone in my room rings: the captain says a Singaporean immigration officer is on board and wants to see me. The officer stamps me into the country without asking any questions — like: "Why the heck are you arriving on a cargo ship?!" A local aboard selling sim cards to the crew says he'll drive me into the city for £18. *Do I like the look of this man?* No. *Would I leave him alone with my sister?* No. *Is he the only way for me to get out of here?* Yes. So I'll give him a go.

Soon after, I'm sat in a van with him — Tony Lee, he says his name is — weaving through Singapore's streets. There's nothing to fear when arriving late at night at a place unknown with no hotel booked. Most will know the word "hotel" even if they know little to no other English. As for guidebooks, they're for beginners; they're travel-by-numbers, a comfort blanket. And are out of date as well: even if it's the newest edition — *Updated for 2014!* — there's a two-year lag from researching to publishing, and a lot changes in a couple of years. The best places — hotels, restaurants, whatever — for today are those that will be in tomorrow's guide-books. To find them, word of mouth is everything, suggestions from travellers, from locals — from Tony Lee.

It doesn't always work out, this wishful rolling of the dice. You hope for the best, but also must brace yourself for the appalling — and appalling is what the Hawaii Hostel is, the place that Tony Lee drops me, a place that seemingly survives on those too weary to be fussy. The receptionist is asleep across the check-in desk. After I wake him, he takes me to an ill-lit rathole without windows. Stains on the walls, scuffs and smears. £25 it costs, but I take it. For one night, I can sleep anywhere. I lay on the sagging mattress and think: I've done it; I've made it to Asia.

SINGAPORE

I'm yet to find a drug that can get me as high as this — and God knows I've tried — gets me as high as that feeling of being at large and lost in a distant continent, among all the strangers, strange in their ways. The rush of freedom; do what I want and go where I want in the unfiltered weirdness of a reality not mine. Eyes open and fresh, peeled with a childlike naivety; the giddy delight of senses sucking up the sights, the smells, the sounds; my mind saturated, broadening. The marvellous oddness of it all; the unexpected, the unanticipated, rAndOmNess. It never gets boring. It's what makes the pains of travel — like sleeping in a cupboard — worth it.

The cupboard I talk of is at The Pod, which labels itself a "boutique capsule hotel", and it's where I check into after leaving the Hawaii Hostel. Its beds are boxed in on all but one side; they've tried to dress them up — light, hangers, fold-out table — but they're basically cupboards. And at £30 a night, not cheap cupboards. But then this is Singapore, the most expensive country in the world — so says *The Economist*.

The Pod, though, is certainly cheaper than the Marina Bay Sands, which my wanderings bring me to. The three-towered gargantuan centrepiece of yacht-filled, palm-lined, glitzy Marina Bay is a 2,500-room five-star hotel for ballers, costs up to a grand a night. It has Michelin-starred restaurants and a casino and a mall — Chanel, Jimmy Choo, Dolce & Gabbana. And across the towers stretches a surfboard-shaped platform; that's a park and a pool — 200 metres in the sky.

Over the web-like Helix Bridge — twisting stainless steel, inspired by a strand of DNA — is the world's tallest Ferris wheel: the Singapore Flyer. A sign says the wheel weighs the same as 437.8 elephants and that the safety net under it can withstand twenty-five elephants falling from a two-storey building. If everything were measured in elephants — an elephant's schlong of apples, a salary of twelve elephants — it would end the miles/kilometres, pounds/kilograms, Dollars/Euros confusion. In a glass pod, up I rise into the heights of Singapore — the city, island, nation, where the spirit of the future breathes. Spread before me, a 21st-century metropolis: a sparkling skyline of glassy slabs, a spaghetti of flyovers, a golf course; a couple of massive biodomes, wonderlands of surreal flora — in one of them, a fucking waterfall; and Supertree Grove: *Avatar*-like structures, up to sixteen stories high — their giant purple trunks burst with vivid flora. There the Singapore Strait, full of freighters; and there Singapore's financial heart, Raffles Place — a ruthless bazaar that hugs the marina, where the banks have erected temples of capitalism, huge, shiny baubles to honour their devotion to the dollar, that dwarf crowds of moneymen and careerists on the make, agents and bankers and stockbrokers, accountants and economists, fast walking and looking worried, jabbering into phones, beetling around.

A city built to the heavens; built so because space-starved Singapore is one of the most densely populated countries on the planet — five million people in a space half the size of London. Built in the sky, and also built on the sea: the country is 20% larger than it was fifty years ago, the sea nearby filled in and built upon. What was the waterfront is no more so. Beach Road, where The Pod is, isn't close to the beach; even if my cupboard had a window, there would be no sea view.

Twenty minutes on the slick subway from Marina Bay is Orchard Road — Singapore's Oxford Street, its Fifth Avenue.

Mall after mall after mall along this 2 km street of swank, more than twenty of them: Paragon and Wisma Atria and ION Orchard, 313@Somerset and Palais Renaissance and Mandarin Gallery. Ferraris parked outside, Lambos and Aston Martins too; inside, frenzied shoppers with Louis Vuitton handbags swipe away, pay their respects to the gods of retail — Marc Jacobs, Hugo Boss, Armani, Cartier, Prada. Malls, malls, so many malls, on Orchard Road in particular, but everywhere; hard to avoid and hard to get out of — like a house of mirrors: every metro exit leads into one, and the exits from one mall take you into the next. At times it feels as if on a layover at the world's largest airport. A day could be spent in Singapore bouncing around the island on the metro, its hundred-plus stations, shopping and sipping Mocha Frappuccinos, without once being in the sun, non-stop crisply air-conditioned to escape the equatorial mugginess.

More shops at the Tekka Centre and Mustafa Centre — open 24 hours a day — in Little India; Serangoon Road between the two: sari shops and shrines, Tamil music blaring, head bobbles and bindis, fresh flower garlands and incense sticks and gold, roti prata and thalis and biryani and tandoori, garish figurines of Ganesha, portraits of playboy Krishna with flute to mouth and milkmaids looking on. A kilometre away, the mood shifts Middle Eastern at Kampong Glam: several streets — Bussorah, Muscat, Arab ... — of palms and hookahs and headscarves, hummus and kebabs. Here, in the 1800s, lived the Sultan of Johore, and the gold-domed Sultan Mosque remains from that time, but this now is Arabia with a modern twist, for as well as carpets from Tehran and Persian perfumes, aromatic Turkish coffee, evil eyes and gems, there are trippy murals and quirky boutiques — flimsy, vintage dresses and flowery shirts — and it's as much for hipsters as for Muslims, with Big Gay Daves taking selfies as common as Farooqs off to the masjid. The Chinese, as well — of course they've stuck a flag in Singapore. Next to the money towers of Raffles Place, terraces of shophouses painted pastels, red and gold lanterns strung across the streets, shrines with gifts for the gods and joss sticks smouldering. The five-storey Buddha Tooth Relic Temple — one of Buddha's teeth there, they claim — and restaurants offering wonton and roasted ducks and steamed buns and moon cakes. For sale at shops and stalls, lucky stones, paper dragons, patterned fans; and at pharmacies: seahorses and pangolin scales and deer penis. I see a display for the Chinese New Year celebrations, which last for fifteen days and are drawing to a close. Born in 1983, I'm a pig in the Chinese Zodiac. Apart from the rat, it's the worst one. If I'd been a dragon, things would have been vastly different. Fame and riches would have awaited. The world would surely have been mine. But as a pig, what chance did I have? People seem to know I'm a pig; I hear it all the time: "You're a pig!" And I think: How did they know that? On the display, advice is given for each sign. For pigs, it says: "Do more sex ... A little chocolate now and then will not hurt."

The rich stew of people in Singapore, its strange brew of Chinese and Indian and Malay, its pan-Asian combo of cultures and cuisines, is because of the British. Led by Stamford Raffles, they rocked up to the steamy, jungly isle at the southern extreme of the Malay Peninsula and said, as the British tended to do back then: "We'll have this." At that time, it was little more than a malarial swampland; only about a thousand people lived here, mostly indigenous Malays. Over the next hundred years, the Brits imported Chinese and Indians, who traded and laboured and pulled rickshaws, worked in plantations and at the docks, slogged at Clarke Quay and Boat Quay, in and out of warehouses, loading and unloading ships from the corners of the Empire, and built buildings typically British: the City Hall and the National Museum and the Old Supreme Court and St. Andrew's Cathedral, all of which I see as I walk Hill Street and Coleman Street, St. Andrew's Road and North Bridge Road, near the mouth of the Singapore River. Grand do those buildings stand still, and images of the colonial past come to mind: cricket on the Padang, Singapore Slings at Raffles Hotel, sandwiches and crumpets, cakes and tea, Rudyard Kipling and Charlie Chaplin swanning around. And that was the case, very much so: the exotic East, legendary Oriental luxury. (Salted with slums and cramped shophouses, brothels and opium dens.)

The heyday of the Empire — until 1942, and what Churchill called "the worst disaster and largest capitulation in British history". Lieutenant-General Arthur Percival was blamed for it; charged with defending Singapore, repelling the Japanese, he had a mare …

"Lieutenant-General Percival, I need a word."

"Not now, Jones, can't you see I'm busy saving Singapore? The Chinks are coming!"

"Chinks? You mean the Japanese?"

"Chinese, Japanese, I never can tell the difference. Shoot first, I say, and ask where they're from after."

"Very good, sir. But I need to speak to you about the Japanese—"

"They'll be here soon. And, let me tell you, when they do come, they'll be sorry they ever sailed to Singapore, to this impregnable fortress. All our heavy artillery is pointed out to the sea, and the moment we spot them, boom, boom, boom! Har!"

"They're here now."

"Fool. Look there: Do you see even one pair of slitty eyes? No, not one; but, by God, they'll be here soon, and when they are, we'll sink every last one."

"They've come by land, sir, via the north."

"Land? By land?! Don't be an imbecile. They can't come by land. They'd have to come all the way through Malaysia. The jungle! Impossible! And it's what, 500 miles? They can't walk that! What do you think they've done, brought an army of horses across with them? Har!"

"Bicycles, sir."

"Bicycles?"

"Yes, they've ridden through Malaysia on bicycles they stole from locals."

"A sneaky bastard, that Commander Yamashita. But never mind, no, no, no, my boy. We've a battalion of Australians guarding the border with Malaysia. You can trust them; salt of the earth are the Australians. They'll do us proud! They'll die for the Queen!"

"It would seem, sir, that they've run off."

"Cowards! Damn them. I've always said you can never

trust an Australian, haven't I? I've always said that. Sissies! The lot of them!"

"So, sir, what should we do? It seems we're in a spot of bother."

"Nothing to fear, lad. We've 85,000 soldiers — good soldiers, great soldiers, British soldiers! The world's finest! Not fucking Australians! And we shall never, never surrender! Never!"

BOOM. BOOM. Shells start falling on Singapore. BOOM. BOOM. BOOM.

"Arghhhhhh. Surrender! Tell them we quit."

That is, pretty much, what happened. A little creative licence, but 30,000 Japanese really did cycle through Malaysia and capture Singapore. And the worst of it was, the Japanese were bluffing; they were greatly outnumbered and had limited ammunition, but they attacked with such sustained ferocity that Percival thought all of Japan had come and brought all of their bullets and shells with them. Yamashita demanded surrender at a point when the Japanese were almost out of steam. Had Percival stood firm a few days more, the Japanese would have folded. A humiliation, the mirage of invincibility vanquished, and the British Empire was never quite the same after that and, piece by piece, unravelled.

Britain regained Singapore after World War II, but by 1965 Singapore was independent, Lee Kuan Yew at the helm. And once on the political throne, he was difficult to dislodge. Twenty-six years as Prime Minister. Then he was "Senior Minister" for fifteen years — outranked in theory by the Prime Minister but still, by every account, the organ grinder. Then, from 2004 to 2011, he became "Minister Mentor". The minister he was "mentoring" was the third Prime Minister of Singapore, Lee Hsien Loong — his son. Few in the world have influenced their homeland's narrative so strongly; he ranks alongside Mandela, Mugabe, Castro. Singapore's merits, its flaws, all trace to Lee Kuan Yew. This a man who said, "I have always thought that humanity was animal-like. The Confucian theory was man could be improved, but I'm not sure he can be. He can be trained, he can be disciplined."

The big stick and the big carrot; that's been his way. The carrot: giddy growth from post-colonial malaise — slums and shophouses, an overcrowded, fractured medley of Muslims and Buddhists and Hindus — to the Switzerland of Southeast Asia. At a time when Communism in Asia was rife — revolutions in China, in Vietnam, in Cambodia and Laos — he bought into capitalism. He ran the country like a corporation — Singapore Inc.; he its CEO — and a wave of wealth followed for Singaporeans, who chomped that carrot with glee.

The stick? Well, in part, a real stick, a stick for caning the disobedient. They cane, they hang. Hang a lot, in fact: it has the world's highest per capita rate of executions. Hangings are for drug smugglers and murderers, and fair enough, you may say; but the fines and canings and shamings, they're for lesser things: Theft or vandalism — canings for those. Littering or spitting is a £240 fine; the same for not flushing a public toilet after use. Begging is illegal. *Playboy* was banned in the sixties and still is to this day. (PornHub, though, is available — a, err, guy told me.) Chewing gum is too on the no-no list. Bring into the country more than two packs, and you might be charged with gum smuggling. Even buying medicines can be troublesome: I'm interrogated at a pharmacy when I try to buy more anti-histamine tablets. The pharmacist says, "You already bought these. Why do you want more?" She knows I bought some earlier because there's a nationwide database of everyone's pharmaceutical purchases, and I had to show my passport earlier today and again now.

I tell her, "I bought one pack, and I've decided I want one more."

"It's too much. You should only take when quiet."

"Take when quiet? What does that even mean? Look, they're just pills to stop me sneezing. I'm not asking for methadone."

"Methadone? Why are you talking about methadone?"

"I'm not asking for it. I'm putting things in perspective."

"Maybe you have a problem with drugs."

She won't sell me any, so I go to one of the Chinese medicine establishments and buy dried donkey testicles to block my leaking nostrils.

The government meddles in other ways, too: there's censorship of movies and TV — no titties or on-screen cigarettes — as well as a media that's muzzled. (It sure helps with re-elections if the media hypes up the good you do and skirts any mistakes.) I met a guy once who printed criticism of the Singaporean government; that didn't end well: A few years ago, I had a month-long flatshare with a couple of randoms, one a 70-something-year-old British journalist called Alan Shadrake. Alan had just written a book, *Once a Jolly Hangman: Singapore Justice in the Dock*, which slammed the Singapore judicial system and included an in-depth interview with Darshan Singh, the state executioner for a quarter of a century. Singh said he'd executed at least 850 prisoners and once hung 18 men in one day. The book wasn't banned in Singapore; it just wasn't there, was oddly missing from bookshops. Alan said he was going to Singapore to promote it anyway, despite being told by the British High Commission that it would be best to steer clear. I'd only known him about three days at that point, and when he said he was off to the airport, I didn't think any more of it — until two days later when I was watching BBC News, and there he was: there was Alan. He was arrested for "scandalising the judiciary" and jailed for six weeks.

On balance, I wonder, is it worth it? Worth the stick to chomp the carrot? A prosperous and manicured, glittering and efficient utopia, the poster child for the globalised twenty-first century, but also a socially engineered antiseptic goldfish bowl, a quasi-democratic Lilliputian cultural desert where to live is only to work, to shop, to eat. Is it worth it? Probably, for most people, yeah, it is. Compare it to, say, the US, the land of the free, where you have a right to say what you want to say, and where you have a right to bear arms, but where people are scared to go out at night. If I had kids, this is the type of place I'd want them to grow up. Sydney, as well, is also a good option, so maybe I'd leave one of the bastards there and one of them here. But as a drug-taker, a gum-chewer, a porn-wanker, a writer of obscene language, a person who pops anti-histamine tablets when he's not quiet, it's not for me. I'm too animal-like.

If Singapore were a person, it would be a supermodel. But every supermodel has an arsehole, and Singapore does too, and I want to look at it (the supermodel analogy there fails). Singapore's arsehole is Geylang, and it's a world apart from the tourist trail, from Marina Bay and Orchard Road, though in distance — as with everywhere in Singapore — little more than a long walk. Its low-rent reputation, its older shophouses and jaded flats, make it a hub for low-wage migrants, workers shipped in from Bangladesh and Indonesia, Malaysia and India, to get their hands dirty at hard jobs the locals reject. Here are the binmen and the brickies, the taxi drivers and dishwashers. As I walk its streets, I see tatty shops and cafes, bars with tables out front at which sit raucous drinkers with buckets of beer, and hear tunes from neon-lighted karaoke joints — "Once upon a time I was falling in love, but now I'm only falling apart, there's nothing I can do, a total eclipse of the heart ..." Very busy, noisy and lively, the seedy, seamy underside of Singapore. Pimps here, tough and tattooed, expressions not to be fucked with, and streetwalkers cruising — on the prowl or perched on benches or leaning on lampposts. Black dresses slitted high; mini skirts and long legs and high heels. They wink at me, make kissing sounds, push out their breasts.

"Take me. Hundred dollar," says one out front of Lai Ming Hotel.

But I don't: My cupboard isn't built for two.

Not a few sinful streets here, but a whole district of places to be massaged or wanked or fucked, which I nose around, randomly cruise. The government, by the way, the so-called goody-goody government, they more than know of this, this Geylang sauciness: The whorehouses are government-licensed. They're in on it, part of the game. The brothels are discreet, not in disguise but not flaunting. No girls on poles in windows, no breasts flashed at those that pass. Left and right, shophouses with doors open; through the windows, glimpses of women on sofas; a few often, but more than a dozen at others. Numbered and patiently waiting to be picked, products on shelves almost, rented by the hour. *No.24, she looks alright. But then, her legs; her legs are fatter than the legs of No.8. But No.8, her nose is crooked. No.11, her nose is a fine nose, but those boobs, they kind of sag ...* They're Thais and Filipinos and Vietnamese, Mongolians and Chinese. No Singaporeans — that's why it's allowed. A foreigner fucking a woman from some other place, well, that's fine; and it's fine too for a bloke from Singapore to do the fucking. But a foreigner fucking a local, oh no, that won't do. Singaporean women are above that.

At one place, I'm handed plastic gloves — to keep the smell off my fingers, they say. And I'm glad I've got them when I delve my hand into the yellow, sticky flesh, and my nostrils are assaulted by a pungent stench, the smell of meat gone off. I push on so as not to seem rude, but it's very, very strange, an oral sensation totally unlike what I'm used to. *Oh dear, is that onion I taste? Christ. And that back-of-the-throat taste, what is that? Cheese? Urgh.* My gag reflex kicks in, and I give up. No wonder there are signs on the metro and in elevators that warn about this — "No durians allowed." — and I wish I hadn't stopped for a fruity snack from a street stall.

On the metro on the way back, a fart forces itself out. (I blame the durian.) Farting on the metro must be illegal in Singapore — I'll be hung for a crime so heinous. So I'll become a fugitive: hide in my cupboard until morning, then escape to Malaysia.

MALAYSIA

KUALA LUMPUR

Singapore, like Australia, is an island, but, unlike Australia, it won't take me months and a thousand pounds to get off it. A bridge. They've got a goddamn bridge from Singapore to Malaysia. If only they'd had a bridge from Australia to Singapore.

I cross the bridge to Johor Bahru — a featureless urban area — where is a smart airport-terminal-like building. I'm through in minutes, provided with a ninety-day visa-on-arrival. It's harder to get into nightclubs than it is some countries. Malaysia doesn't mind if you're wearing flip-flops, or say, "Too many lads already." From here, I'll go to the capital Kuala Lumpur, 350 km away. I find my exit at a bus station nearby — Larkin Sentral — where is a constantly changing line-up of fancifully-coloured vehicles in various states of ruin; signs in their front windows display exotic-sounding destinations: Negeri Sembilan, Selangor, Melaka. Here, it feels more like Asia. I've left a realm of order, and the feeling of foreignness is amplified. Poorer here, dirtier and noisier than Singapore, more chaotic. It's heat, it's dust, it's horns and engines. It's music from crackling speakers, and it's shouting into phones and at people. It's touts, and it's hawkers, and it's moneychangers. It's a raucous commotion and general rabble on the hustle — "... Buy this ... Give me money ... "

At a couple of dozen counters lined along the front of the station, swarms of shabby blokes sell tickets, harassing everyone who passes. I trust anyone, typically, who doesn't tingle my spidey-sense, but at bus stations — the domain of thieves and deceivers — I trust no one unless they have a halo. I scout for the most religious-looking ticket-seller, thinking they'll be least likely to rip me off. They won't risk a stint in the eternal hellfire just to rinse me of a few extra ringgit. I spot a woman in a headscarf with worry lines so deep that they must be the result of living in constant trepidation of displeasing an imaginary overlord in the clouds — she'll do.

"I'd like a ticket to Kuala Lumpur, please."

"Go to KL, ticket is £6."

"And the bus, how is it? It's a good bus?"

"Bus is super nice."

"TVs? A toilet?"

"No TVs. No toilet."

"So why is it super nice?"

She points — straight-faced — to a photo of a bus with "Super Nice" written on its side. It's the name of the bus company.

While I search for the super nice bus, a call to prayer sounds from the station's PA system and nearby mosques. Malaysia, like its neighbour, has a mix of Malays, Indians, Chinese, but here it's the Malays with the majority — not the Chinese — and Islam is the official religion. They're not religious fanatics, not the nutter-types that fly planes into buildings, but most women wear headscarves, and there are some in head-to-toe Muslim dress. Two of the latter stand outside the station chanting: "Work, work, work for humanity! Work and give your money to the Palestinians!" They hand out flyers to those who pass but not to me. I either don't look like someone who works, or I don't look like someone who gives a damn about humanity. (Let me tell you, I *do* work — sometimes. As for humanity, no comment.)

A four-lane highway for a few hours, then the bus drops me at Puduraya, an old bus terminal in the centre of KL —

as the locals call Kuala Lumpur — and from there I wander
to find a hotel, then set off to see the city ...

I prowl, walk the sultry capital sweating, looking for
nothing in particular but also looking at everything,
searching for what makes the city. I walk through Bukit
Bintang; see there streets of run-down apartments with
paint peeling and washing hung on balconies; see there
luxury hotels and fancy restaurants and western-like pubs.
Some of its streets, the run-down and the swanky are side by
side or on top of each other. On its main strip, Middle
Eastern eateries and well-heeled tourists from Saudi Arabia
and the Emirates, strolling, shopping, smoking shisha. The
shopping at a multitude of mega-sized malls: At nine-storey
Plaza Low Yat for pirated software and obscure adapters and
refurbished MacBooks, and at dated, utilitarian Sungei
Wang Plaza for shoes, purses, clothing, luggage; Muji and
Zara and the like at the polished Pavilion, and within the
biggest of them, Berjaya Times Square, a fucking roller-
coaster. I see mom-and-pop stores and 7-Elevens, and a
monorail and raised, covered walkways and red sedans —
"Teksi" signs on their roof — honking the snarly traffic.
Women offering reflexology massages but dolled up like
prossies; I see them and think wankology massages are
what's really on offer. I pass carts of fruits and juices —
mangosteens and tamarinds and lychees, melons and
longans and rambutans — and in grungy alleys see grotty
restaurants, lots of greasy old-style ones; they look shite —
the tables stained, the floor littered — but the food, oh dear
Allah, the food looks sublime: trays of curries buffet-style,
the sauces yellow, orange, brown, red, and plates of nasi
biryani, mee goreng, roti canai. And I see some vendors
practically juggling tea: the milky teh tarik — "pulled tea" —
poured back and forth from head height between a couple
of jugs, the liquid falling like a waterfall from high to low,
over and over, to froth and cool the tea.

I leave Bukit Bintang, walk beside freeways with terrible
traffic, along palm-lined streets of grubby prosperity and
characterless buildings, through the unpretentious, organic
jumble that is KL, which feels to me a scruffy, beaten-up
Singapore. And it shouldn't be a surprise, any similarities to

Singapore: KL had the same ingredients as its neighbour: the British overlords, the medley of Chinese and Indians and Malays; it's just the recipe that's different. I walk along Jalan Tun Sambanthan, the main thoroughfare of Brickfields, where the buildings are painted brightly and in windows are colourful sweets and saris, and walk along Jalan Petaling and Jalan Tun H.S. Lee in workaday Chinatown, past its shophouses and temples, its stalls of t-shirts and watches and handbags and electronics, its stores of knick-knacks and general bric-a-brac, and look at the faces, the very many faces, of KL's two-million-people pick 'n' mix, the faces of the street vendors, the sleeping tramps, the security guards, the smiling schoolgirls ... Nameless, they are to me, and faces will soon enough be forgotten, but it is they, the thousands I see as I walk, that form the jigsaw of impression.

I ride the Kelana Jaya line — part of KL's patchy railway network — to Dang Wangi station and walk from there to the KL Tower: a 421-metre white toothpick with a bulb near the top that rises from the only virgin rainforest that remains in Kuala Lumpur. It's the world's fourth-highest telecommunications tower, I find out. A very crappy claim to fame. The world's fourth-highest tower: fair enough. The world's highest telecommunications tower: also fair enough. But the world's fourth-highest telecommunications tower is like me saying I'm proud of being the world's fourth-best under the age of fifty UK writer of overland travel books that are mildly funny and occasionally offensive. Still, I'll go up it, as it's the duty of a person in a foreign country to go up tall things. I don't know why — why if there's a high building or mountain in Malaysia or Belize, the traveller must scale it — but that's just one of the laws of life, like Thou shall not kill, and it must be done without question, and I'm thus obliged to go up the world's fourth-highest telecommunications tower.

After I pay, a woman hands me a form and says, "You must sign this before you go up."

"Sign a form? What for?"

"BASE jumpers come here every September. You must sign to say that you're not a BASE jumper. BASE jumping is only okay in September. Please, don't jump today."

"Do you get many BASE jumpers going up in flip-flops and without a parachute?"

"No."

I sign the form — what a waste of a sheet of paper.

It takes a minute in the lift to reach the open-deck summit of the tower, where are 360-degree views — and chest-height barriers around the edge, and signs that say: "Caution. High-risk area." I look out at the hazy sky, look out at the bird's-eye views of KL, the minarets and skyscrapers, the Titiwangsa Mountains in the distance, the reckless urbanisation and the furious traffic snarl-ups on the freeways. Binoculars up here, which I use to spy: Among the concrete and the crowds, the frenetic activity of this city, I pick out people scurrying around Chinatown, haggling with taxis, taking photos of the world's fourth-highest telecommunications tower; and I pick out people on balconies drinking coffee, and see through apartment windows into living rooms. (It's only voyeurism if I have an erection, right?)

I don't need the binoculars to see what I've seen all day from wherever I've been in KL: the city's showcase landmark looming over the skyline, a 450-metre sci-fi-like behemoth: the Petronas Towers. Like silver rockets, the shimmering, tapered 88-storey towers are iconic — and surpass expectations. Built in 1998, they're still the world's tallest twin buildings. They'd look the part in Shanghai or Singapore, look better than New York's World Trade Center did. At 417 metres, the World Trade Center was the world's second tallest twin towers. Some redneck in Arkansas probably believes Malaysians flew that plane to take out their nearest competitor. It's impressive that Malaysia, a country that plenty of people — especially rednecks in Arkansas — couldn't place on a map, has the world's tallest twin buildings; and even more impressive that from 1998 to 2004 these were the tallest buildings anywhere on the planet. Throughout the twentieth century, the US had a firm grip on that title; then Malaysia — "Bro, is that, like, near Iran, where them other ragheads are?" — stuck up its towers and stole the crown. Since then, first the Taipei 101 became the tallest in 2004, followed by Dubai's Burj Khalifa in 2010. Proof, if you want it, that money and power have shifted eastwards in the twenty-first century.

The Petronas Towers came with a hefty price tag: over a billion pounds. You might argue that they should have spread that money around. What they did was like going to the shops fully intending to purchase a bunch of stuff, stuff you need like pants and jeans and shirts, but instead splurging everything on a three-foot top hat with shiny trimmings. In 1995 came the KL Tower, and soon after in 1998 the Petronas Towers; since then, the bold statements of intent dried up. There are a few other modern ornaments around KL, and at the right angle it's quite futuristic with the towers and the eleven-station monorail. But zoom out, and it's a faded metropolis that feels past its prime already, and it's certainly a sloppy second to Singapore, a shittier remix of that city.

Perhaps, though, it's not past its best, but just enduring those years of awkward adolescence. Because it's still young, only 150 years old. For a city, that's nothing: London is 2,000 years old. A blink of time ago — the late 1800s — it was a mere tin-mining settlement carved out of the jungle, just a muddy encampment at the confluence of a couple of rivers — the Gombak and the Klang. And that's what Kuala Lumpur actually means: Muddy Confluence. When the British made it the capital, it was still a dingy outpost, a wooden shantytown; then settlers began to pour in, miners and labourers and merchants, dreaming of fortunes from tin. *Tin!* As if there was money in tin. *Great riches!* It was the Apple stock of the day. Later, rubber boomed, became the Bitcoin of its time. *Rubber!*

Progress, no doubt, but it will be a while before KL is on anyone's bucket list. With Bangkok to the north and Singapore to the south, it's the overlooked middle child. And fairly so, for it's an urban sprawl that no one needs to see. To visit here instead of Singapore would be like opting for Cardiff over London, and even the most diehard Welshman — Dafydd Griffiths, a sheep farmer from Teifi Valley near Llandysul in Carmarthenshire — wouldn't do that.

From there to KL Sentral station to take a train to Batu Caves. It's an attraction that because it's in a foreign country and has a funky name, I'll go to. The UK has plenty of wonders I could easily visit but haven't. The Lake District, I've never been to; not ever considered going to. But if it were in Zambia and called Wilaya ya Ziwa then I'd go. Like going up high things, it's a rule of travel — No.75b: If a thing in a land afar has a name that soundeth funky, then go you must to visit that thing. (Which is why Ayers Rock was rebranded as Uluru: to tempt more people into an 800 km out-of-the-way roundtrip for a fucking rock.) At Batu Caves, jagged and forested limestone thumbs stick up. Within them, sacred caves that house a temple and shrines. At the foot of the steep 272 steps that rise into the caves, a towering golden statue stands guard, the Hindu god of war: Lord Murugan. Aided by a can of Red Bull, I climb the steps; my heart pounds like an amphetamine-fuelled drummer as I reach the top, where are incense-wreathed shadowy caves. Through an opening a hundred metres above, strobes of sunlight bathe a candy-coloured temple. Beside it, some tossers have tainted the sacred setting with a store that sells flashing picture frames and "Hinduism way of life" car stickers. Cock-a-doodle-doos echo from unseen chickens, and there are monkeys — monkeys marauding everywhere; monkeys with mangy fur and evil eyes. I'm not scared of monkeys, but it's not a fair fight. They can bite, scratch, whatever, but if I kick a monkey, someone will video it and upload it to YouTube: "Evil man beats innocent monkey." And that'll be the end of me. I once witnessed a friend stabbing a monkey with a fork, but he had a get-out clause in that we were sat at a table eating fried fish and his baby was with us. That fish was tasty, really excellent, and I suspect he'd have stabbed that monkey even if there was no baby with us, but the baby being there would have meant something in the kangaroo court that is YouTube comments. I have no baby, so slapping a monkey with a flip-flop, I'd be the devil incarnate. *Guilty! Cancelled!* Yet these monkeys, they really need a slap. A guttural growl from one, which then leaps onto a woman's backpack. She screams. The monkey grabs a water bottle from the side of the bag, then races off. Another steals a bottle of Gatorade straight from a bloke's hand. Once they've drunk their plunder, they toss the bottles on the ground, so they're litterers as well as thieves. Next time I'm online, I'll donate to L'Oreal. More monkeys than people here now, but back in January, tens of thousands of people were here for the annual festival Thaipusam. At dawn, they start at a temple in the centre of KL; then an S&M-like parade from there to here. Devotees skewer their flesh, or wear frames with dozens of spikes that poke them as they walk, or carry heavy milk jugs atop their heads that hook into their skin. And these guys are on foot all the way — seven hours — not taking the KTM Komuter like I did. Why? Why this macabre procession? As penance for their wrongdoings. If they do this once a year, the gods will let go that time they pulled a sickie, or that other time they slept with their best mate's wife, and even that time they stabbed a monkey with a fork.

For dinner, I opt for a bowl of beef noodle soup for £1. But to call it "beef" is generous; from a cow, yes, but not the bits you'd want. This, I think, is brain-and-bollock noodle soup, tarted up with a little chopped spring onion. It's rank, but I'll eat it anyway because I still believe what my Mum told me about not wasting food when Africans are starving — even though I think a starving African would think twice about this. Halfway through the meal, someone tells me, "Your chopstick upside down." In Asia, this is looked upon like an Asian in Europe using a knife and fork upside down. Would you think an Asian sat next to you at Nando's using a knife and fork upside down was an idiot? You know you would.

As I'm forcing down the final "meatball", onto the scene appears a sorrowful sight to see: An elderly, slightly stooping woman, her clothes tattered, limps in off the street in bare feet. Her face is sickly and sad; her black hair needs cutting. Her crutch scrapes across the floor as she goes from table to table.

To give, or not to give; that is the question. A question a traveller is asked daily in Asia.

Some strain to not see nor hear; blank the unfortunates into the background. Others put down their iPhone for a second and search for a coin or two to give the beggar, the cripple; then off they go, off into the cruel world, thinking they're Mother Teresa while they're shopping for souvenirs or sipping a mojito. Me, I want to shove her out; out of this restaurant, but really out of existence because she reminds me of *all* the sick and the hungry, the desperate orphans, the destitute, the cripples, the deaf and dumb and blind; *all* the poverty, *all* the wretchedness in the world, *all* the misery, the terrible, terrible misery, on a planet that should provide amply for us all, not just the lucky or unscrupulous bastards that make up the few. How many people suffering right now in KL, in Cairo, in London — my own supposedly prosperous country; how many asleep on the streets, crammed in shanties; how many abused, bullied, or addicted to booze or drugs; how many with Alzheimer's, with cancer, with crabs, how many wasting away; how many is it all too much for, about to throw themselves off a skyscraper or poison their bodies with pills; how many ... What a shitty world.

It's savage out here — on this tiny rock that's hurtling around the galaxy — but the truth is if you allow the misery, the unfortunates, to weigh on your soul, you'll drown. And what's the point in that? It's a problem for governments, not for drifters like me; that's my say on it. A dick, you may call me, to not give some coins to her. But, I say, I'm not ruthlessly indifferent; it's just economics. If I give to her, what about the bloke outside without arms? The blind child down the street? What about all the beggars in Thailand, in Burma, in India? And, a few ringgit, anyway; what can she do with that? Buy some soup, yeah, but in a few hours, she'll be hungry again, back where she is right now — and the cycle repeats. So I'll leave it to governments, the governments that splurge on things like the world's fourth-highest telecommunications tower, when instead they could buy homes and soup for all.

I return to my room at the Cube Hotel — £17 per night — in Bukit Bintang. My room is larger than a cupboard but doesn't have any windows. I'm staying here not because I can't cope with sleeping in a cupboard or roommates pissing on the floor, but because — with my passage through Australia lasting for weeks longer than expected and the grand spent on the cargo ship — I need to do some online work to top up my funds. It requires quiet time, which is in short supply at hostels. With a laptop and wifi, I can work from anywhere. Usually, that place is in bed. Don't jump to conclusions: I'm not a webcam gigolo that strips for pervs. (Though I would be for the right price. Email me at mark-walters@email.com with offers). I'm an SEO consultant, helping businesses rank their websites higher in Google. With hocus-pocus trickery, I manipulate the "organic" search results and push a bunch of cowboys to the first page for, say, "Bristol vending machines" or "best dentist in Doncaster". So some advice: Don't trust Google — especially if you're in Doncaster and need a dentist. But most people are unaware of this — don't know that Google is outsmarted by chancers in their pants in bed in KL — and so when they search on Google for "best book" and find this very book, they'll think this book is better than *To Kill a Mockingbird*, or *Pride and Prejudice*, or *The Great Gatsby*. About that, they'd be wrong. (If that's you — if you Googled "best book" and as a result bought this book — I'm sorry.)

GEORGE TOWN

Back to bunks and sharing. One of those I'm sharing with is a snorer. I know snorers can't help snoring, but I don't care: they need to have big S's branded on their foreheads and be forced to sleep in the streets. The place itself — House of Journey — is a bargain at £6 a night, but at that price, it comes with flaws: When I turn on a tap, a full-on brown spray comes out. And for over forty people, two bogs only. *Two!* And one of those is a squatter — a doored cubicle around a hole. With a nasi lemak breakfast burning through my bowels, I can't wait for the proper toilet to free up, so I settle for the squat one. I've used them in the past, and it's always a stressful experience. Crouched over the chasm, your knees crack and creak. You wobble every which way as you try to balance without touching any surfaces. Beads of sweat stream down your face as you try to hit the oh-so-small target knowing that the slightest miscalculation will result in the nightmare scenario of shitting into the jeans around your ankles. With the deed done, you have to clean yourself using not tissue paper but a hose pipe or a bowl of water. I'll get a lot of practice at this: from here until Europe, at least half the toilets I come across will be squat ones. I haven't ruled out the stress-free alternative of wearing diapers.

George Town is 350 km up the west coast from Kuala Lumpur, on the small island of Penang, twenty minutes on an old-style rusty ferry across the Penang Strait from peninsula Malaysia, from industrial, unattractive Butterworth — which is the opposite of George Town. Here, the past is still the present, and it could still be decades ago. I walk its steamy streets — Lebuh Chulia and Lorong Stewart and Jalan Chowrasta, Lebuh Campbell and Lorong Pasar and Jalan Hutton — seeing an eclectic mishmash of centuries-old architecture (some colourful beauties, some weathered, decaying antiques with blistered, peeling paint) and seeing Chinese characters scrawled large in gold, in red, and seeing old fellas on sputtering motorbikes as aged as them, and palms and plants in this place that's humid and green, in this place where it shines and it rains all year. Up and down the streets I go, past the rows and rows of two-and-three-storey nineteenth-century shoulder-to-shoulder shophouses which are the fabric of this town. Stretches of them — thousands, probably — a jumbled assortment of cafes, laundries, work-shops, restaurants, and guesthouses, that are yellow, white, green, blue. Some showy, with louvred windows and carved timber doors; others shabby and functional, with flaking plaster and brickwork exposed, with full-width folding doors open to the world, with dust-coated ceiling fans stirring the heavy air. A place of old and a place of food, where woks flare and grills sizzle at humble restaurants and rickety kerbside hawker carts. Char kway teow, hokkien mee, assam laksa, and other exotic dishes served. A place too of art; its walls canvases for eccentric murals — there's a Tyrannosaurus attacking a teenager on a motorcycle, there's Bruce Lee kung-fu kicking cats. It's crack for selfie-hungry narcissists.

At some dusty ground on Lebuh Armenian, I stumble on a flea market. A couple of dozen locals have each laid out a sheet to display their tat on. And it really is rubbish — beyond second-hand and onto third and fourth. Despite the paucity of anything of value, buyers — who are outnumbered by sellers — scrutinise objects like they're buying a diamond. One seller's wares consist of a rusty can, a light switch, a piece of rope, a pot lid (no pot), a used paintbrush, a book (in Russian), a certificate for something, a World Cup '82 plastic whistle, and a KFC alarm clock (batteries not included). And down by the water at Weld Quay, I come across shacky villages on creaking wooden piers, a stone's throw apart. Each belongs to a clan: Chew, Yeoh, Koay, Tan, Lim, Lee. In the 1800s, Chinese immigrants arriving in Penang would join one of these clans to help establish themselves in their new country. They all fished, and the clans would battle each other for the best spots to fish from. It was like *Game of Thrones* but with more fish. I walk the length of the largest — Chew Jetty — past seventy-odd tin-roofed, open-fronted wooden homes, and see old men in old vests watch old films on old TVs, and see fish gutted and washing being hung to dry, and see small boats moored, bobbing in the green sea. They still fish, the descendants of the settlers that still live here, but that's more of a side gig now; cash from tourists, that's the money-spinner these days, selling souvenirs and snacks, so they can augment their arsenal and finally eliminate their nuisance neighbours and reign supreme on the fishy throne.

That's the curse of a blessing from UNESCO, which George Town got in 2008: Men who fished now sell fridge magnets and postcards. Shophouses previously home to rattan weavers and tinsmiths are now coffee shops and hostels and art galleries. A place becomes a zoo; the locals monkeys to be photographed. It's "saved" but at the price of planeloads of Singaporeans demanding tall double shot decaf espressos, and hordes of *Lonely Planet* disciples in same-same-but-different vests and comedy sunglasses: "I went to, like, India, and it was, like, totally amazeballs." That said, it's not too bad here; not yet, at least. Lebuh Chulia is the main street, and its only brand name shop is a tiny 7-Eleven. But even if it does go full-on mainstream, it's preferable to the residents than the stresses of poverty.

One man thankful to UNESCO is Mr Seng. He rides one of George Town's ubiquitous timeworn trishaws. There's one wheel at the back, above which Mr Seng sits to peddle, and two at the front, either side of a seat for two. It's rusting but brightly coloured, is decorated with plastic flowers. Mr Seng is sixty-something years old. I ask him, "How long have you been doing this?"

"More than thirty years."

As he rides me around — straining on the pedals, dripping sweat — I feel somewhere between a colonial governor surveying the empire and a toddler in a pushchair. Progress is slow. He's not even close to the speed limit. I want to whip him like a horse with my earphones to quicken his pace, but there are too many backpackers around, and they're liberal-types likely to report me to Amnesty. We ride down Jalan Masjid Kapitan Keling, a road where multiple religions in peace reside: Set on a fine lawn, white St George's Church, with its Greek-style columns and octagonal steeple; then the lions and dragons and candles of the smoke-wreathed Goddess of Mercy Temple; a little further on rises the lurid tower of the Sri Mahamariamman Temple, detailed with comic-strip-like scenes from the scriptures — devils and deities and cows; and at the end of the road stands the Masjid Kapitan Keling, its black domes and white arches, its call to prayer for the Muslims of George Town. On we ride through Little India: Piles of fresh coconuts and baskets of almonds and cashews; goldsmiths and flower stalls and stores selling incense and aromatic soaps. The Lakshmi Video Centre, on the corner of Jalan Pasar and Lebuh King, with Tamil movie posters donning the walls — all quiffs and shades — and CDs and DVDs for sale: "Original, sir, very, very good!" And outside the temple, ash-daubed priests in white loincloths standing sipping milky tea. Then, along Beach Street, we ride to the remains of 18th-century Fort Cornwallis — rusted cannons on its walls, aimed towards the Strait of Malacca; to the Padang, a large lawn once used for cricket and military exercises, now for dog walking and jogging and picnics; to the stately, white City Hall and the grand, collonaded High Court — both handsomely standing for over a century. And, on Lebuh Farquhar, to the colonial-era grande dame the Eastern & Oriental Hotel, where stayed Noel Coward and W. Somerset Maugham.

The British influence on George Town is clear. That name, for starters: George Town sounds as Malaysian as Grimsby does. And there's the street names — Campbell and Stewart, Hutton and King — and the church and the obviously European-looking City Hall and Eastern & Oriental Hotel, as well as some corners of the place that look a little like London backstreets. This was the first place the British settled in Malaysia, and, for a while, it prospered through trading cinnamon and nutmeg, opium and silks, and it may have soared to the heights of Singapore if Singapore weren't so near. The founding of Singapore marked the start of the end for George Town; in effect, it became George Town 2.0 and sucked people and trade from it. As Singapore woke up, George Town went to bed — a long slumber that lasted well into the twentieth century and that preserved it as an image of a past age, an image of the Singapore flattened by the wrecker's ball. If not for its UNESCO listing, it would still be disintegrating into the dustbin of history. That listing changed everything. A new chapter.

As for the first chapter, by now I've used up all the lines I say to all locals wherever I am — "Such a great country! ... The food, the people, wonderful! ..." and Mr Seng and I stray onto that — history, the British — and he says, "Malaysians accept that it's in the past, but it's not forgiven." We talk more, and at some point he mentions Burma, and I ask what Burma has to do with anything, and he says, "The British took over Burma as well."

"Did they?" I ask, surprised.

He's shocked that I don't know. "Don't they teach you this at school?"

I run through what I patchily learnt in history classes: World War II, maybe World War I, the feudal system, Shakespeare (or was that only in English, and not history at all?), the Romans and the Normans and the Vikings, the suffragettes and the spinning jenny, a selection of Henrys, Oliver Cromwell, The Battle of Hastings, a bit about dinosaurs — though there I might be confusing cartoons with history class. No Burma. Very little Asia, if any at all. And I got a B at GCSE, so it's not like I wasn't paying attention. Sure, I could have put more effort into studying history, could have taken history as an A-Level, could have attained a first-class degree in history from Oxford or Cambridge, could have dedicated my life to learning all the history, all six million years of humans being on earth; but if you've ever met a historian, you'll know they're boring bastards. No one wants to be that guy. And it's not that I'm simply dismissive, an arrogant ancestor of a former empire. I just don't know history — even my own. I don't know the names of my great-grandparents. What I was doing in 2003, I've no clue. Did I have a job that year? Don't know. Was I in the UK? Don't know. The nineties, which was after I was a little kid but before I guzzled a bunch of drugs, that's the period I know best: The death of Princess Diana, Oasis v Blur, Euro '96. (History that's largely useless except for in a pub quiz now and then.) So I just muddle through. The facts in this book, any history in these pages, I know only because I Google it on the day. Without Google, I'd be lost. Ask me who Alexander Fleming was, and I'll offer guesses ranging from mass-murderer to the last king of Scotland, to the lost, fifth member of The Beatles, to the inventor of the steam locomotive or the lightbulb or cheese; before finally, in defeat, asking you a question: Who the fuck cares?

So, no, I haven't rote-learned a catalogue of colonial crimes so I can travel around apologising for arseholery from a century or more ago. About that, I'm not sorry. My country has blood on its hands, yeah. Yours too, most likely, unless you're from somewhere irrelevant like Canada. But, at some point, the past has to be let go, and when no one who did the deeds back then is still alive today, that point has passed.

But I opt against such a rant at this nice guy, so I just say: "Oh, yes, they do teach us that, but I was, um, off school that day, um, ill."

My history teacher Mrs Thompson definitely didn't teach me how George Town got its start, but Google did and here's that story ...

In the 1780s came Captain Francis Light, an adventurer employed by the British East India Company; came to an island that was then "one vast jungle" with "a population of only fifty-eight souls". He didn't take the island by force; no, he made a deal with the Sultan of Kedah, who ruled this part of Malaya at that time:

"That island, I want it. The Dutch have set up in Sumatra, have a port there and a minimart and a cheese shop, and so we, we mighty British, need to set up in these parts too."

"That island? You mean Pulau Pinang?"

"Yes, that one. But Pulau Pinang? What kind of a name is that?"

"It means Areca Nut Island."

"Ridiculous! Absurd! It'll have to be renamed. Let me think ... Prince of Wales Island!"

The Sultan of Kedah stifled a laugh.

"So your Nutty Island, how many magic beans do you want for it? A hundred?"

"We don't accept magic beans. Not after last time."

"A hard bargainer! Ok, you win: a hundred and ten magic beans."

"No, really, we don't want magic beans."

"A hundred and fifteen?"

"No."

"So what do you want?"

"Well, there is one thing: It's a little problem we have with the Siamese; you see, our neighbours to the north, they're threatening to invade. Could you help with that? Use your army to fend them off?"

Captain Francis Light paused for a moment, thinking that he had absolutely no authority to make a deal like that. Then said: "Deal! We'll send you a thousand soldiers, a million if you need them, should those dastardly Siamese ever darken your doorstep."

"Excellent. If you could just sign this contract, then the deal will be done."

"Contract?! An Englishman never signs a contract. The word of an Englishman, everyone knows, is gold — solid gold! An Englishman has never, never ever, broken his word. I swear it, swear it on my mother's life, on the life of King George, swear it to God Almighty himself; and even to your Allah — I swear it to him too. In your hour of need, we'll be there right by you, shooting those Siamese fuckers dead."

"Well, ok, if that's your custom, then I'll take your word

for it. Here are the keys to Pul- I mean Pricks of Whales Island. The bins are collected on Wednesdays."

Time passed; the Siamese invaded.

"Mr Light! They've come, they've come! The Siamese are invading!"

"The who are doing what?"

"The Siamese. They're invading our land."

"So? What's that got to do with me?"

"Our deal. We had a deal. You know, you got the island, the island you're on now, and, in return, you said you'd protect us from the Siamese. A thousand soldiers, you said. Up to a million."

"Did I? Sure it was me? Sure it wasn't a Captain Francis Might you made a deal with?"

"It was you. It's not like we get a lot of Englishmen coming here and taking our islands. It's something I'd remember."

"I really don't recall that at all."

"Well then, the island, how did you get it?"

"I bought it fair and square. Paid a man a hundred magic beans for it."

"No. I was that man, but I refused the magic beans. The deal we agreed was the island for military protection."

"A contract? You have one as proof of this alleged agreement?"

"You said we didn't need a contract. You said an Englishman never breaks his promise; you gave a whole speech about it. You swore on your life you'd shoot them all dead."

"Now I know you're lying. I never, never, never swear on my own life. I'll swear on anyone and everyone else's life, but never on my own."

"But—"

"Look, I feel bad for you, with your land being invaded and all that, but soldiers, no, I really can't send any. The boss, old Charlie Cornwallis, he wouldn't be up for that at all. But I'll tell you what I'll do; I'll give you some—"

"Please, no, not that. We don't need that. We need soldiers, not—"

"Magic beans."

The Sultan never got the agreed military aid, but Penang stayed in British hands and was for a time the eastern frontier of the empire. Sydney came two years after George Town, and Adelaide forty-eight years on from then. I've not-so-subtly shoehorned Adelaide in because it was founded by William Light, son of Captain Francis Light. With the father and son link, it was decided in 1973 that Adelaide and George Town should become sister cities. What does it mean to be sister cities? I had a look to see, and, according to Adelaide's official website, the most recent celebration of their sister-hood was in 1993: "Following the success of the South Australian television show *Postcards*, a segment called 'Postcards from George Town' was produced." So in short, it means not very much at all. William Light's son, there's no record of his following his grandfather's and father's steps in founding a settlement. I guess he saw the world's biggest rocking horse in Adelaide and thought that civilisation was complete.

Back at the hostel, the talk is of a plane missing, presumed crashed into the sea: Malaysia Airlines Flight 370 from Kuala Lumpur to Beijing. There's a rumour that rednecks from Arkansas hijacked it as revenge for 9/11 and planned to take out the Petronas Towers but got lost as the only map they brought was a street map of Little Rock. No plane crash worries for me on this trip — it seems improbable that one will crash on top of me. A road accident, though, is more likely than usual. Malaysia is a road death hotspot, making the top twenty in the list of countries with the most road fatalities per year, per hundred thousand inhabitants. Thailand — where I'll go next — is fourth on that list.

I speak to a Chilean staying in the same room as me, and he asks what route I'll take to Europe.

"Thailand, definitely. Then maybe Burma to India; and from there, I suppose, Pakistan or China. "

He recently went to Burma and tells me, "There are restrictions on where you can go, and they change week to week. There are many military checkpoints, and if they don't want you to go to a particular place, they'll kick you off the bus. The Bangladesh border is closed. The borders with

India and China are open, but you need special permits to cross them. As a foreigner, you've no chance of getting one."

I don't want to hit a dead-end in Burma and have to backtrack into Thailand. So I rework the route I just made up: Thailand to Laos, then ... China? I'll roll with that until I'm told I can't.

THAILAND

AO NANG

It was two hours by minivan from Butterworth to the Thai border at Padang Besar; there, a small town, a simple crossing. Then onto dull Hat Yai an hour away, and five hours further to Ao Nang: a town on the west coast of southern Thailand, in the province of Krabi. For the ride to Ao Nang, the driver seemed to be engaged in an unofficial attempt to break the world record for most people in a minivan. There were seats for fifteen people, but through knee-sitting and innovative limb-positioning, he crammed in twenty-five. If we'd had an accident — not unlikely based on the white-knuckle driving — paramedics would have been pulling people out for days (like a twisted version of a magician pulling rabbits from a hat).

On Ao Nang's white beach, the surf breaks benignly; fifty-plus long-tail boats line the shore, bobbing up and down with coloured cloth tied around their bows, on which their captains recline and beam bright smiles beneath aviators. I wade out to one of the boats, the past knee-height water giving my jeans a slight clean, and pay £2 for the ten-minute ride to Railay, a peninsula inaccessible from the mainland, and we're soon motoring along the sea.

A few foreigners on the boat; one is chatty Isabella, a

hippy granny from England. I guess her to be well over sixty, but she says she's just fifty-three. She wears a black-and-white bandana, smokes a fag. She says she has leukaemia; says she hates monkeys, says she hopes there aren't any at Railay — they've got AIDs, she says. "I don't want that as well." Her son was in Mensa at six years old. Her ex tried to poison her. The staff at her hotel keep calling her sir. She says she's twice told them that she's a madam, not a sir, but still they call her sir. She looks at the scenery and says it's just like Phi Phi Island: the palmy coast and the jungle and the limestone cliffs. "I went there eighteen months after the tsunami in 2004. I had hallucinations: I could see the tsunami happening, people trampling each other to escape. I was in non-stop tears and had to leave after a few hours." She might get a massage this evening, she says, and she hopes it's not like the one she had in Sri Lanka. "A vaginal massage — well, that's not what the sign on the door said."

Railay is the type of place shown in glossy brochures. On long, dark north evenings, in drizzly November, it's this that's dreamed about. It's not a secret, but it's not "a place"; not full of cement and plastic and neon. No cars here, and no roads either; just dirt tracks, jungle footpaths that twist and turn and rise and fall. On the paths, I wander around Railay's beaches: West Railay, for the wealthy wanting luxury; East Railay, for the cheapskates wanting a pancake and banana shake; Phra Nang, for the everyman wanting to lounge and swim; and Ton Sai, for the cool kids wanting to climb and toke. While foreigners are in their skimpies — with thunder thighs and moobs on show — locals keep as covered as possible: to avoid getting tanned because they think light skin is more sexy than dark. They stare bemused at foreigners lying in the sun, burning their lovely white skin. Dumbfounded foreigners stare back at them, sat in the shade applying skin-whitening products. Like the Thais, I keep myself covered, but for a different reason: wearing shirts and jeans every day has given me freaky tan lines. My face, arms, and feet are all brown, while the rest of me is white. (Except for my willy, which is light brown because sometimes I walk about with it hung out of my jeans.)

I settle on Ton Sai as the best for me, and I return there

on a path through the jungly centre of Railay, where are monkeys up trees eating papayas; some with palm-sized babies clung to them. On the way, I see a tree with more than a hundred flip-flops nailed to it; a sign says: "The flip-flops on this tree were collected around Ton Sai in 26 minutes in the 2013 flip-flop-athon. What do you consider rubbish?" It breaks my heart that these flip-flops were abandoned. People buy them impulsively, thinking them cool and fun. Then, after a couple of weeks, as their holiday draws to an end, the prospect of wearing them to the office dawns on them, and so, under cover of darkness, they bury them in the sand. Cruelty of the worst kind. Flip-flops are for life, not just for holidays.

At Ton Sai, the jungle comes right down to a long sweep of soft sand. No hotels on the beachfront, just a few shacky restaurants serving shakes and fried rice. Backpackers rolling joints; others clinging to sheer cliffs. I speak to one, and she says she works at a rock climbing centre in Chiang Mai. "It's for my Masters. I'm helping them implement technology into their business."

"Technology? Like escalators?"

"No, I mean, like, a website and booking system."

Right now, not too many backpackers. They're off at the once-a-month Full Moon Party on Koh Phangan, 300 km from here. I debated going, and it would be on-brand for me to go, but I've been before, and it's the sort of thing you definitely need to do once but don't really need to do twice. When I went in 2005, I lost my shirt, my flip-flops, my wallet. I cut my foot on glass and got badly bruised in a chest-slapping endurance competition with a rugby player from New Zealand. I stripped down to my boxers for a 2 am swim and sucked on a ladyboy's nipples. And I did two pills and magic mushrooms, which might account for all of the above.

No, better to leave that to twenty-three-year-old Mark and let thirty-one-year-old Mark be here. And so I sit for an hour, doing nothing but savouring being here: deep in the tropics on this palm-fringed, powdery sand, looking out at the fishing boats in the blue bay, at the rocks rising sharply and cloaked in green. I couldn't be happier.

Back at Ao Nang, I walk the main strip of tour shops and

money changers and pharmacies and minimarts, of stores selling t-shirts, bikinis, shades, souvenirs. German, Russian, and Scandinavian families and couples eat spaghetti, steaks, and tacos at air-conditioned, glass-fronted restaurants with names like Eden, Roma, Gringos; and Indian suit-sellers line the road, trying to shake the hand of every passer-by: "Hello, my friend. Suit very nice. Please, yes, thank you." It could be any tourist destination, anywhere. The main difference, aside from the happy-ending-optional massage shops, is a narrow, neon-lit lane: RCA Entertainment, says the sign above its entrance; on the sign too are silhouettes of a few busty ladies. I walk down the lane, where are bars — Amy's and Kitty Bar and One More — with loud beats and lights flashing, and where are women in low-cut tops and hot pants and miniskirts and high heels, pawing and screeching and trying to drag men into the bars — "Hello! Welcome!" Other women are sat like a harem, giggling and preening. "Handsome, sexy man, come, come, come ..." It's mostly women, but there are also gay men and trans girls. I don't see any women dressed as fellas, but if that's what you want and you're willing to pay, someone would meet your need because anything goes in Thailand. It reminds me of Blur's *Girls & Boys*:

"Girls who are boys,

Who like boys to be girls,

Who do boys like they're girls,

Who do girls like they're boys,

Always should be someone you really love."

But in Thailand you don't have to love them; you just have to give them £20.

I pick a bar and sit down and order a beer for £1.50. In seconds a woman is sat by me.

"Name Yaya. Name you?"

"Mark."

"You France?"

I've heard that before, and every time I hear it, I'm not sure if it's an insult. I say, "No, England."

"Age you? Thirty-eight?"

"Thirty-eight?! No, thirty-one."

"Buy me drink?"

"Look, I don't want sex or any of that stuff. But maybe you can tell me some stories; you know, funny stories about the sorts of guys you get here, about some crazy situations you've been in. So how about that? I'll buy you a drink if you tell me some stories?"

"You buy drink, yes?"

"Yeah, a drink for some stories. Deal?"

"Yes."

So I buy her a drink — a "lady drink", which is twice the price of my drink.

She takes a sip, then smiles at me.

"So, stories ..." I say, and I settle in for stories of depraved and debauched behaviour, of whips and orgies and golden showers, of forty-year-old virgins and blokes with one-inch cocks, the whole gamut of sexual craziness from this warrior of the trade. (Not because I'm a pervert, but because I know that some of you are, and I want to give you what you want.)

She laughs. "You funny."

"Well, some people think so. But what I want is funny stories from you."

"Name me Yaya."

"Yeah, I know, we've done that."

"You England?"

"Yep, like I told you before."

"Thirty-eight?"

I start to think that she doesn't know English beyond the absolute basics of name, age, etc. And that thirty-eight is either her favourite number or the only number she knows.

I say, "Do you know much English?"

"Yes." And she smiles.

But I'm not convinced she understood the question. It's the sort of thing I do when someone asks me something in a language I don't know: I just nod and smile. (And then end up going to a wedding of someone I've never met or eating something that shouldn't even be fed to a dog.)

I ask her, "What's the name of this town?"

"Yes."

"What's the square root of 169? And I'll give you a clue: it's not 38."

She nods, then leans closer: "Me like you. Me, you, fucking?"

I try again with another woman. I give her the drink, then say, "So, stories ..."

"Man come drinking. Then fuck-fuck with lady."

"Ok, right. But that's basic stuff. Give me the crazy stuff."

"Just that happen. Drinking. Fuck-fuck."

Great. What a story. I'll get that typed up and posted off to Spielberg.

I still have money in the meter, so stick at my questioning, but get nothing usable. It's like talking to one of those dolls that speak when you press a button on its back — "I want pee-pee." But this one would have to be returned to the manufacturer because it keeps asking you to fuck it.

I'm soon left alone as it's a pay-as-you-go system: as soon as their drink runs out, if you don't buy them another, then they're on to the next guy. Which is fine. I know the routine. It's not my first rodeo. They're salesgirls, and what they're selling is themselves. If they don't smell a taker, then why waste their time on him? And I'm anyway pleased to not have to talk. I've come to watch; the women a little, but more so the men, who for the most part are ugly and overweight and middle-aged. Whites and Indians and Chinese and Japanese, but mainly sunburnt Europeans. They play pool with the girls, and play Jenga against them, and play Connect Four as well; play not so much for fun, but so they don't have to talk so much. The girls flirt with them, tell them they're handsome and strong and funny. There are kisses and fondles, but no one strips. It's mild debauchery, not the last days of Rome with dicks and fannies out and at it like rabbits. That will come later — back at hotel rooms — and is the whole point of all this. Which is why, I guess, whether or not the girls speak English is neither here nor there, really, because everyone speaks sex.

The guys think it a heavenly Happyland; here at this lane, but really the whole country — and Ao Nang is, in fact, low-key for this sort of thing; this is non-league compared to Bangkok. That they're out of shape or balding or seventy-three or have a one-inch dick is no strike against them as it would be at home, and any slob can score in Thailand. The girls are pretty and cheap and everywhere, and to bag one is easy. It's the women, indeed, that do most of the hunting; they're the wolves. Packs of them laid in wait, primed to pounce on the suckers passing through, ready to bleed them of their cash. The poor local women exploited by predatory foreigners thing isn't true a lot of the time. It's, at best, a half-truth. They're mostly in control, pulling the strings of the foreign muppets. The less attractive he is, and the less experience with women he has, the better a mark he is. The recently-divorced middle-aged "gentleman" is most coveted. He comes on a two-week holiday and meets what he thinks is a simple-minded floozy at a bar, and for a fortnight, they "date". They do all the things a normal couple would do: they go to the beach, they dine at decent restaurants, they sleep together at the end of the day. Then, after a fortnight, he goes home, and the relationship continues online. He plans to come back in 3-6 months, and there's even talk of getting married. He'll send her money, so she doesn't have to work in a bar any more — and also for any extra things that pop up, like her fridge that's broken or her father's sick buffalo. Win-win, right? He's in love, and she's saved from prostitution. Except that he's not the only one saving her from prostitution. The bloke who landed in Thailand the day after the last one left, he's also saving her. And after that one flies back to Munich or Copenhagen, a new white knight flies in from Barcelona or Barnsley.

I know this not because one of the fuck-fuck dolls told me, but because I've spent time in Thailand teaching English, and it's common knowledge to anyone who's spent more than a few months in the country. And a friend of mine, Jason, was at one point even writing emails to a woman's many men. He was in Thailand on what was supposed to be a three-month journey around Southeast Asia, but he landed in Thailand and spent the whole time here: partying and sexing the locals. He was twenty-four and a fine-looking fellow, so he didn't need to pay for sex, but he just happened to hook up with a girl who worked in that scene. Which, by the way, is the way it is for the cool and the young and the handsome; the local girls just like them and want to be with them for a good time. It's the sad and the old and the ugly that have to pay. So, Jason, he ends up at a city called Pattaya — the Champions League of whoring — and he's seeing this girl day to day, but it's nothing serious, just a couple of young people having fun, and each day she had to spend an hour-or-so writing emails to her men. She had a bunch of them all over: One in Switzerland, another in the UK, a newly-acquired Australian who thought they were getting married next year ... And they would all send her money every month — the Swiss guy, about £1,000. She could speak English alright, but not write it well, so she asked Jason if he could help her out by writing the emails for her. So he'd be there at her fancy apartment, and they'd wake up after a heavy night of drink and drugs and sex, and she'd make breakfast while he'd log into her Hotmail and send off sexy emails to Zurich and Liverpool and Melbourne and wherever. And these blokes would be tugging off to these emails from their rescued sweetheart, blissfully unaware that right at that moment their rescued sweetheart was having post-brekkie fuck-fuck with Jason.

But Thailand's reputation for this sordid business is overstated. Of the thirty million that come to Thailand every year, maybe 10-15% — an unscientific estimate — come for sex. The rest come for all the great things Thailand offers — "Such a great country! ... The food, the people, wonderful! ..." Still, that foreign demand for prostitutes, added to plenty of demand from local fellas, results in a quarter of a million hookers in Thailand. It's illegal, but the police are paid off. It's good for the police, and pretty helpful to the country, as the cash that goes to the women passes along to the poor regions of Thailand, particularly the north where farming is the primary industry and £3 daily wages are common.

The second bargirl I spoke with, that's precisely her situation: from the north, family to support — and likely the same for Yaya as well, though I couldn't even get that info from her. A daughter selling sex — £20 per night from a customer; and much, much more if she can sign him up for a monthly subscription — can easily support her whole family: her mother and her father, her lazy brother and her drunken husband and any children she might have, and the cousin she hasn't seen since she was six ... She's sacrificed for the benefit of the rest.

Not her first choice career, but in her position, the smart move. She sells what best pays, and what sells best is her body. It's a job. She puts in a shift like a nine-to-five office robot who sells not his body but his mind and time. We all sell something to earn a quid or two, and who's to say one sort of selling is better or worse than the next. In the girls' position, I'd do what they're doing. Faced with being a farmer or a labourer, I'd be a rent boy. Poke me, piss on me, do as the fuck you want with me, so long as I don't have to be out in a field sorting mangoes — "Good mango, bad mango, good mango, bad mango ..."

After a few beers, I go to get food and find that a couple of kilometres further along the strip, there's less of a Costa Del Thai vibe. I come across a market selling cheap Thai food. For £1, I buy rice and beef cooked in spices and herbs. It comes in two bags, which I take to my room to eat. Once there, I realise there's no plate or cutlery. The solution: tip one bag into the other and use a bottle top as a spoon. This works better than you think it would — try it at your next dinner party to minimise washing-up.

There's no solution, though, for the power cut. As I sit in the dark and scoop food into my mouth with a bottle top, I wonder if I should have just had a taco at Gringos.

BANGKOK

I arrive in Bangkok — or to give it its full name: Krung Thep Mahanakhon Amon Rattanakosin Mahinthara Ayuthaya Mahadilok Phop Noppharat Ratchathani Burirom Udom-ratchaniwet Mahasathan Amon Piman Awatan Sathit Sakkathattiya Witsanukam Prasit. I travelled here on a very pink — inside and out — first-class bus. £13 well spent. A stewardess handed out blankets and snacks: a carton of juice, a couple of little cakes, and a sandwich with a picture of a chicken on the package but a jam-like filling. (It tasted of neither chicken nor jam.) My seat reclined and had a massage feature (press a button and I'd get a gentle shaking), and between my seatmate and me, a couple of armrests, so I didn't need to battle him for it; that I was happy about, as I was sat beside an orange-robe-wearing, shaven-headed monk. I thought it wasn't very monk-like to take the first-class bus when there were cheaper second-class ones. And he drank Sprite, not water. If he's serious about being a monk, he should have walked and drunk his own piss.

It's 4 am when I get off the bus at Mo Chit Station in the north of the city. There's a Skytrain station 2 km away, from where I can ride into the centre quickly and cheaply, so I start walking there, out of the station and along a busy highway — for Bangkok never totally sleeps. I go a few hundred metres when a motorcycle zooms past, then slows; the driver turns to look at me, then continues slowly and again turns his head; he then rides on for fifty metres and pulls over and gets off his bike and ducks behind a row of phone booths. I stop and pause, spooked by his behaviour. The road is busy, but there are no other pedestrians. And if he plans to mug me, he's picked a good time: as well as my laptop and my iPod Touch and my passport, I've got £250 of Thai baht on me. Normally, I'd just Tombstone the bastard, then walk on — because, you know, I'm that hard — but after twelve hours on a bus (even one with a seat that reclined and massaged), I'm not at my best. My peak time for wrestling is after 3 pm when I've had a good lunch and a nap.

Maybe you're thinking he's just a kind fellow wanting to offer me a lift. To that, I'll offer you a little story ...

I once before accepted the offer of a lift in a situation similar to this: A bloke on a motorcycle stopped ahead of me. I hopped on, and within seconds of us speeding off, his hand reached from in front and tried to feel my dick. I swatted away the hand, but back it came. And again. He wouldn't stop the bike, and I resorted to rocking side to side to try to make us crash; slowly at first, then quite violently, and that was enough for him to stop — after he'd had a fourth lunge at my cock.

So this man now, this man hiding behind the phone booths, I don't know if he wants my wallet or my willy, and at 4:15 am, I don't fancy a chat with him to find out. So I do what I almost never do: flag a taxi.

I tell the driver "Asok", which is the centre of Bangkok, and for the 10 km drive there, I stare out the window, stare out at the Big Mango, the City of Angels, Krung Thep Mahanakhon ... I stare out at the sprawling concrete jungle, the ugly, dense tangle of bulky flyovers and broken pavements; the tousled power lines that criss-cross the city and that look like evil spiderwebs; the eight-lane highways strewn like spilt pad thai and the heart-sinking blocks of bleak flats — worn and patched and botched; most still dark, but some lights on, some unlucky bastards starting to stir. And I stare out at the fast-food joints and petrol stations and elevated billboards — skin-whitening products, "Study Australia!", Krungthai Bank — and at the dark forest of condo towers and multi-storey car parks and shuttered shopping malls. Little in the way of slums, but also little exotic. Some temples, some green amid the asphalt and concrete, but most of what was green has long been gobbled up by developers.

"Massage?" the driver asks me, as along Sukhumvit Road we ride. It's a question a bloke alone in Bangkok is asked every day, by taxi and tuk-tuk drivers, by whispering blokes in the street. The question is "Massage?" but the question is really "Sex?" I tell him no, but he still gives me a sleaze safari, drives me around the backstreets of Sukhumvit Road, where even at this hour, sauce is spurting. It's bars and clubs and "short-time" hotels, and it's neon and scuzzy and raucous, and the roads teem with tarts and pervs and drunks and grinning devilish faces, necking bottles of Singha and smoking cigarettes, slurping noodles and spewing and pissing. We pass NANA PLAZA — "The World's Largest Adult Playground" — a mall of smut from where sounds a discordant jumble of music, and where, I know, are girls on poles, swaying and grinding, and girls in bikinis or topless or nude; like zoo animals, those girls, on stages that act like cages, and all of them — as well as the bar staff and the cleaners — are available for takeaway fucking. Filth in there, and also on the streets and the bars that line them: waiting taxis, spilt trash bags, chattering whores, and drunk motorcyclists; a wild-eyed, butch transvestite combing her curls, and a humpback selling gum and candy and condoms from a wooden tray. There are "freelancers" stood along the road, tapping on their phones — the rough-as leftovers not yet picked. Several dressed like they're off to a prom, and others to the beach. "I go with you," one calls to me when we're stuck in traffic. There are fat, pink fellas with small, pretty girls, and there are ladyboys that look like ladies, and ladyboys that look like blokes. There are elderly saddos and whooping Americans, the obese and the balding and Indians with moustaches, and dead eyes and crew cuts and rattails and Russians, and blokes with sandals and pulled-up white socks. There are whorish-looking women and girls as fresh-faced as college students; there are ones that look like models and ones that look like the after-photos for cosmetic surgery fails. Some are dressed as schoolgirls, others as bunnies or angels. They're eighteen, twenty-five, forty-eight, and Thai or Laotian, Burmese or Cambodian — it's not a career that discriminates. Offers made — "You want boom-boom?", "Me go with you?", "Fuck-fuck?" — and negotiations played out ("No, not do for 500 baht. I tell you, 1,000.") and people doubled up with laughter and people slumped in doorways. It's raunchy, garish, sad: the flesh trade in flow.

The taxi drops me at Asok, and I find a hostel nearby called 3Howw — not a typo: no space between the 3 and the H; and a double w. It's a cupboard-place like in Singapore; this one, £9 a night. I could get a room in Bangkok for that price, but I prefer a better location than the extra space and privacy. Where I am is where intersects the Skytrain (BTS) and subway (MRT); from here, I can easily cross the city — the city of ten million vehicles, of streets jammed bumper-to-bumper. Notorious are its traffic jams, and it's no hyped-up exaggeration. I can't check in to the hostel until midday, but they let me hang out on a bean bag, which I do until the city wakes to the day, and then I walk five minutes to the MRT and ride it two stops — Petchaburi and Phra Ram 9 — to the Chinese Embassy. I'll go to Laos before China, but for Laos I can get a visa-on-arrival at the border. The Chinese, though, aren't so kind; it's one of the countries that doesn't give visa-free or visa-on-arrival access to Brits. We stole Hong Kong and flooded their country with opium, but that was ages ago. Come on, China, get over it.

I hate embassies — always a ball-ache. Forms and photos and photocopies, and the people that work at them are often dicks. Service with a smile is a motto not applied; unnecessary because however much the service sucks, you have to suck it up. What they're selling — entry to their country — isn't sold anywhere but here and other equally unwelcoming places (and those places are all over a thousand kilometres away).

As well as a completed application form — that took me a couple of tedious hours to fill in — the following are required:

- A detailed day-by-day itinerary.
- Hotel booking confirmations.
- Inbound and outbound plane tickets.

I've plotted a route to take me through a few Chinese cities and into Kazakhstan; noted down tourist-related activities and sights in those cities; found train times that fit with the route; booked hostels on booking.com (which offers a free cancellation policy). The plane tickets requirement, I'll have to explain myself out of.

At the drab, grey visa wing of the embassy, I sit on one of the plastic chairs and settle in for a long wait, feeling worried. I'm screwed if I don't get this visa. If I can't travel through China, I'll have to either travel from Burma into India — which I've been told is basically impossible — then get a boat from India to somewhere in the Middle East; or get a boat from Thailand to Russia. The latter might be possible but would likely cost four times more than the boat from Australia to Singapore. My funds won't cover that cost.

When it's my turn, I go to the counter and push my wad of papers through a hole in the glass — so low that I have to bend nearly ninety degrees to talk through it. The short, rotund Chinese woman on the other side — who speaks abruptly in broken English — spends a couple of minutes looking through the papers then quizzes me on my work status and lack of flights. She's satisfied with my answers but then throws an unexpected spanner in the works: "Xinjiang province is next Kazakhstan. It have problem now with China central government. If you want go Xinjiang province, you must letter invitation from

Xinjiang province government. No letter invitation, you no get China visa."

I ask, "How can I get a letter of invitation from the Xinjiang province government?"

"You must to contact them. Phone. Email. Up to you. Not our problem."

"Do you have contact details for them?"

"You want, you find. I tell you already: not our problem."

There's no chance I'll get that letter of invitation. I imagine a phone call to the Xinjiang province government going like this:

"Hello, I'd like a letter of invitation."

"Ging gang, goolie goolie goolie goolie, watcha, ging gang goo, ging gang goo."

"Oh, err, sorry, does anyone there speak English? I need a letter of invitation, so I can visit Xinjiang."

"Eh? Pren crackey?"

"No, not prawn crackers. A letter of invitation."

"Me no noey you. Fucky offy."

I leave the embassy and consider my options: I can avoid Xinjiang by travelling northwards through China into Mongolia then Russia. Or lie about my route on the visa application and slyly travel westwards through China, through Xinjiang into Kazakhstan — the more direct, cheaper option. I'll sleep on that, return tomorrow.

From the embassy, I walk a couple of kilometres along Ratchadapisek Road — an eight-laner; essentially a motorway through the centre of the city — to the canal stop at Saphan Asok. This is Khlong Saen Saeb, a canal that slices the city from east to west. There were once many canals in Bangkok, but now they are few; the old ones were "modernised" — filled in and paved into roads. They're serviced by powerboats (sort of canal buses) that dock at a stop-off for a minute. People flood off and pile in: A few white faces, but this is for locals, really, for commuters from the suburbs: schoolkids, suits with iPhones, secretaries in heels. A boat comes, and I pay £0.20 for a seat, and we power noisily along the canal, through rancid, murky water that's foul with detritus: plastic bottles and bags, polystyrene, abandoned flip-flops, coconut husks, a bloated dead cat; past walls of graffiti and chainlink fences, past the rear of office buildings and mouldy tenements and luxury condominiums, and past too the canalside communities — slums, some may say — that face onto the water: patchwork houses pieced bit by bit over years, and lopsided wooden homes with rusty roofs.

I'm off the boat at Hua Chang, and a few minute stroll along a lane — a soi, as the Thais call them — takes me to Siam, the very centre of modern Bangkok. In 1962, this area was a shantytown; from that then to now being Bangkok's heart: this its Leicester Square and Piccadilly Circus and Oxford Street rolled into one. Here is MBK: eight-hectic-storeys of suitcases and trinkets, of soaps shaped like penises and elephant-print cushions and iPhone covers, of thousand-year-old hand-carved Buddhas made last year in China. Here too the one-percenters at Paragon, browsing Louis Vuitton, Versace, Prada — a Lamborghini dealership in there too — and Central World, full of brands familiar to foreigners: Fred Perry, TopShop, Marks & Spencer. And there are the concrete, hulking pillars of the BTS; this station the only one at which its two lines cross. People backed up haunch to paunch for the climb down the steps from it, a motley funnel of sweating humanity bumping elbows, buzzed on caffeine and the energy of the place. Thousands trooping onto the streets, droves of human cattle filing into the cacophonous broiling tangle of Siam. The sidewalks jammed with rows of parked motorcycles and lined with boutiques, nail salons, dental clinics, beauty stores, language centres. Food hawkers everywhere — fishball noodles and sweet potatoes steamed and yellow mango with sticky rice — and I see monks in orange and police in tight, brown uniforms, and students in white and blue — the schoolgirls with their skirts down to their ankles, and the uni girls (who in Thailand still wear uniforms) with their skirts nearly up to their waist. "Pretties", as they're called, are here too, in short, flashy dresses, marketing promotions, and also the blind and the short of a limb and a man with his face burnt horribly. Another bloke, his body twisted and misshapen, is lying face down on a skateboard with a begging bowl in one hand and is using his other hand to grope slowly along the sidewalk, looking like he's an urban surfer paddling through an asphalt sea.

From Siam, Sukhumvit Road rolls out to the east from the centre to the suburbs, with the Skytrain trailing the length of the clogged, broad artery. Traffic aside, it's the strip of Bangkok that could be Singapore. It's the bow on the city's shabby, chaotic wrapping; it's modern gloss. Sukhumvit is Thailand's most famous street, but its first paved street — the first to be paved in the whole country — is five stops away on the BTS: Charoen Krung Road. All the roads in Bangkok, the city infamous for congestion, for its confusion of cars and buses and motorcycles, and it all started right here with this one. I get off the BTS here at a station called Saphan Taksin that's beside the Chao Phraya River — a poisonous-looking river that slices through the west of the city, and that's busy with barges and ferries and long-tail boats. Just over from the station, where Charoen Krung Road meets Sathorn Road, is a 47-storey "luxury" condominium. Well, 80% of one, and the last 20%, that must be the luxury portion because the 80% is a lofty, eerie carcass, windowless and derelict. The Sathorn Unique is its name; and the "Ghost Tower" as well, for how it looks and also because it's allegedly haunted. Locals say the project was cursed, and there are two theories as to why: it casts a shadow on a nearby temple; it was built on an ancient cemetery. The more business-minded might blame the 1997 financial crisis in Asia: The baht lost more than half its value, and the local stock market dropped 75%. A real estate market booming collapsed; hundreds of high-rise projects were abandoned. Since then, most have been completed or demolished, but still a dozen-or-so rise into the city's smoggy skyline, post-apocalyptically. So here it stands rotting, the Sathorn Unique, its gaudy hodgepodge of curving balconies and Corinthian columns, its escalators to nowhere; here it stands as a ghostly, skeletal monument to economic disaster. A lesson learned, you'd hope, but Bangkok is sprouting now as it was back then, cranes and construction projects all over, funded by credit and optimism, the capitalist dream, and all old seems precarious, a contract away from being a skyscraper or condo or mall.

But Charoen Krung Road for now is still old — a sense of Bangkok in the seventies. It runs for 9 km, and runs roughly parallel to the sinuous curve of the Chao Phraya River, and is low-rise and lined with a muddle of shop-houses stained and grimy. Along this road and its side streets are florists, grocers, and opticians, and old-school mom-and-pop shops, and cramped, packed stores stacked high with fabrics or stationery or electronics, and shoe shops and motorcycle repair shops, and ones full of TVs and PlaySta-tions — teenagers playing *FIFA*. There are ducks hung from their necks in glass cabinets, and ladies toiling over grills and woks, and monks among the scoffers and shoppers, among the schoolkids and the pensioners. There are gem shops — jade, rubies, emeralds — and open-fronted, battered workshops, and old coin sellers and lotto ticket sell-ers, and sellers of amulets (little carved Buddhas worn for luck) and men selling pineapples and mangosteens. A rice porridge place — Jok Prince — open for fifty years, and a 103-year-old Chinese restaurant offering wontons and crabs, and vendors wheeling by with vegetable pushcarts, and bicycle-based hawkers selling papaya salad or coconut ice cream topped with corn and red beans. Here also are paper shufflers and salesgirls lunching al fresco: sitting on plastic stools at fold-up tables on sidewalks, eating oily chicken rice, eggy mussel pancakes, stir-fried crispy pork belly with kale, talking over the screeching brakes of buses a metre away, over the noisy swarms of beeping motorcycles.

Along Charoen Krung Road I walk — and as often in Bangkok, I have to zigzag around obstacles; its sidewalks obstructed by motorbikes, by hawkers, by stools and para-sols (got to stay out of the sun!), by trees, plant pots, ice boxes, by gas canisters and signposts and electrical boxes, by poles, pillars, bollards — and near the end of the road is Wat Pho, one of the oldest and largest temples in Bangkok, and a leafy pocket of tranquillity, a calming oasis in this hectic, cement metropolis. Its showpiece is a copper statue of a naked lady. No, it's not; it's Buddha, it's golden — always is. This one, though, is larger than the norm (46 metres long and 15 metres high) and is reclining, lying on one side — built that way, I guess, to save on paying for scaffolding. I sit at the rear of the hall and look up at the gilded Buddha. The chants, the incense, the goodness, sweep over me, and his heavy-lidded stare on me, I say a prayer — which is more like a wish-list: "I'd like cash, good luck ... oh, and that visa for China, I really, really need it." In return for what I ask, I make all the right promises: "I'll be a good boy this year, Buddha, very good indeed; better than I was all the other years, which, yes, is a low benchmark." I sit a while longer, thinking about all the gold; the gold at this temple, the gold at the jewelled and glittering temples all over Thailand; thinking that it's an odd choice for paying tribute to Buddha, whose schtick was simplicity and minimalism. Siddhartha Gautama (as he was called before the rebrand to Buddha) was born into wealth; he was an aristocrat, or even a prince, some say. He had it all. Had it all and decided he didn't like that life, so gave it all up to live like a hobo. So these palace-like temples, I don't think he'd approve. And Bangkok in general, he'd curse — if he hadn't given up cursing to be enlightened. For all its temples, the notion of Bangkok as even slightly spiritual is laughable. It has more 7-Elevens than temples. It has more prostitutes than monks.

From there, I take a pink-and-blue tuk-tuk. We go only a metre before the driver turns to me and says, "We go suit shop?"

"No."

"Buy gem?"

"No."

"Massage?"

"No."

A bumpy, jerky ride, slow through the sluggish churn of cars, takes me to Khao San Road: a scruffy 400-metre street of fleabag guesthouses, boxy, thin-walled cheapies for £4 a night, of travel agencies, currency exchanges, restaurants, and drinking joints, that's rammed with 40,000 sweaty tourists boozing, dancing, eating; and buying baggy trousers and tie-dyed beach dresses, and bartering for handcrafted wooden frogs and I-Sucked-Cock-In-Bangkok t-shirts, and browsing shelves of bootlegged bestsellers with smudgily printed pages. There are signs for fake IDs, for sim cards, for massages, and carts of fruits and mounds of noodles and

spring rolls, and stalls of fakes and knick-knacks and handicrafts, of belts, watches, luggage, purses, shoes. Tables and
chairs set up roadside; the eaters sharing the sidewalk with
rats and cockroaches and scabby cats, and dripping sweat
from the spice and the sticky night air. Others eat burgers or
kormas or kebabs, or are sat on the kerb eating skewered
grasshoppers, scorpions, beetles. They eat, and they drink;
drink banana shakes and towers of beers, and some are
guzzling cocktail buckets — whiskey with Red Bull and fuck
knows what. They drink at bars — like LUCKY BEER and
Khao San CENTER, two places that face-off over the street,
and whose DJs are duelling with volume — but for all the
bars, it's really a street party, many drinking and dancing in
the road, throwing shapes and bobbing heads to hip-hop,
techno, and cheesy pop, and singing along to live bands: "It's
my life, and it's now or never, I ain't gonna live forever ..."

There are "pretties" peddling Singha, Chang, Leo, and
there are tuk-tuk touts: "You want sexy show? Lady very nice.
Ping-pong?" One is trying to persuade some Germans to go
to a place called Super Pussy. There are also, among the
clothes and tourist knick-knacks, pornos, knives, tasers.
Drugs too: "Sale: Valium 1.0, Oral Jelly, Cialis, Kamagra &
Viagra. Prescription not required." They do swift trade,
savvy tourists knowing that Bangkok is best tackled by
taking valium in the morning and viagra at night.

Lots of hair-braiders and tattooists, and there are more
Indian suit-sellers than there were in Ao Nang — "Hello, my
friend. Suit very nice. Please, yes, thank you."

From behind a rack of tacky t-shirts, a fortune-teller
pounces: "Mister," he says, "I can look your palm and tell
your future."

I say, "If you look at my palm, you'll tell me my future is
to wash my hands."

"Really, mister, if I look your palm, I can see many thing.
Even name your mother."

"I'm not paying you to tell me the name of my mother. I
already know it."

The road is a dog's dinner of man-buns and bandanas
and backwards baseball caps, of vests and beards and tril-
bies; a jumble of braids and dirty t-shirts and bare chests, of

the very white, and the very tanned, the very drunk, and the very, very drunk, of Italians and Brazilians and Australians, and people speaking Chinese and Spanish, Tagalog and Hebrew, Korean and Hindi. It's a people-watching extravaganza: the good, the bad, and the ugly — the bandaged casualties of motorbike accidents and the ladyboys on the prowl for a catch, the guys sucking from balloons ("Laughinggas! 100B") and the wounded whiskey tipplers carried out of Brick Bar and 999 WEST (the bars the Thais prefer).

A good many here are a year or two out of uni. They once would have spent a summer Interrailing, June to August on Europe's trains. Now it's Southeast Asia, is Thailand and Cambodia, Vietnam and Laos. They party in Bangkok; then they bus it to Siam Riep to party there; then they take a flight to Saigon, and there they party. They talk a lot, but not about Thailand, nothing of its culture. They talk about partying. They say, "Mushroom Mountain, that was fucking crazy ..." They say, "I was so pissed at Siem Reap, I never even saw Angkor Wat ..." And when talking about Luang Prabang, a temple town in Laos, they say, "The after-hours place there is a bowling alley!" Plenty of rhapsodising and hyperbole and trumping others' tales — "A snake bit you? Two snakes bit me!" — as they make new pals ("I just loooove your dreads!") and as they reacquaint: "It's you! You! You remember? Hanoi! That was wild! I can't believe it's you! Wow, this is like fate, destiny. It's unbelievable! I never thought I'd see you again. You! Oh, it wasn't you."

There are those at the end of their trip, who, after three months in Southeast Asia, are noisily opinionated, cocksure, and wise, who, because they've been to Vang Vieng, think they're Neil Fucking Armstrong. The wisest of the wise now walk barefoot and smoke roll-ups, and should be avoided at all costs. Also, there are the just-arrived, weighed by brand new backpacks too large: They have a *Lonely Planet* and a hairdryer and two changes of clothes per day, have an iPod and an iPad and an iPhone. They have a tent, they have malaria tablets, they have a Swiss Army Knife (a gift from their father) — but won't use any of them. And some have pens or stickers to hand out to the "poor". At least a few of them — though they don't yet know it — will wake in the morning with an ill-fitting three-piece suit, a tattoo on their forehead, and a raging hard-on.

Those here are just some of the millions per year that come to this city; this city of hawkers and monks and tuk-tuks, and also of hookers and beggars and scammers. They come to this place of ping-pong shows and noodle shops, ghosts and temples and temptations, motorcycles and "Massage?", where the choked streets and spiderwebs of sois are aromatic with incense and sewage and grilled pork, and they're dazed and jammed and dehydrated, suffocated by the crowds, the traffic, by the frenzy and the free-for-all. It's terrible in many ways. Few landmarks and the noise is atrocious. It's hot, it's dirty, and it's chaotic, and it's stinking and disordered; its air is poisoned and polluted are its waters. Yes, lots of reasons for complaints and headaches, and those used to package holidays in Greece or Spain might think it a dreadful, greasy, seedy place, an insufferable, primitive capital.

But you can have an espresso for breakfast, get your teeth whitened, learn how to salsa. It's hardly backwards. And while Singapore is cleaner, is quieter, is nicer, it's not seductive or anarchic or *sanuk* — a Thai word for fun, jokes, silliness. There are cities that feel alive, and this is one of them. And so they come, and come in their millions; come to the colourful horror show that is Bangkok. Because though it's awful, they love it. And so do I.

CHACHOENGSAO TO MAHA SARAKHAM

I reworked my visa application for a route that takes me through China into Mongolia and, a week ago, went back to the embassy. I dealt with a different woman at the counter, who, after looking through my application, asked to see my visa for Mongolia. I said that I hadn't got it yet, that there was no point getting it if I couldn't get a Chinese visa. She again inspected my paperwork, then handed me a pink slip and told me to come back in a week to collect the visa. That was progress, but I knew the visa still needed to be signed off by someone higher up the chain, who may want to see train tickets — not just dates and times — and a visa for Mongolia.

Today, I'm again back at the embassy. I arrive there at 6.45 am and am second in the queue. The guy in front is an agent with lots of forms and passports. He stinks of booze. If I had to come here every morning, I'd turn to booze too. It still somehow takes me three hours to get back my passport, but the wait is worth it as I open it to see a Chinese tourist visa valid for twenty-five days from the date of entry. Great news, but my entry into China isn't guaranteed: The visa for Mongolia, not only do I not have it, but I'm not going to get it, as that's not the route I'll take. Yes, I lied about my route on the visa application. At the Laos-China border, they may demand to see that visa for Mongolia and turn me away if I don't have it. If they do let me in — and I've no idea if the odds are in my favour or not — I'll go off-piste and do what they told me not to do: head to Kazakhstan via Xinjiang. I'll do that and hope no one checks on me while I'm there, realises I'm somewhere I'm not supposed to be, and locks me up.

I return to the hostel to pack, then catch a minivan to Chachoengsao, a town an hour east of Bangkok. In 2009, I spent a year teaching English at the town's uni. I was paid £650 a month to teach half a dozen three-hour lessons a week. The university has a couple of campuses, and it's an hour ride on a bus to one of them. I hated buses so much that I quit the job despite it otherwise being a cushy gig. The irony of that now, when I spend more time on buses than bus drivers do.

A Filipino called Mae that I worked with at the university has set up a makeshift language centre in the back room of a shop. It's not obvious what type of shop it is: in it are two rails of clothes and an empty bakery counter. There's also a stack of mushroom tea in the corner, which is Mae's other sideline business. She swears these particular mushrooms prevent cancer. She's asked me to help out for a lesson, thinking that the parents will be pleased to see a white face. (Teaching in Thailand is that superficial.) I have three years of teaching experience, but the last of those was more than four years ago, and all of them were teaching twelve-to-twenty-one-year-olds. Today I'll teach four-year-olds. I don't like kids that little: they have a ten-second attention span and can pee their pants at any time. The class starts with me sat on the floor and the kids seated in a semi-circle around me. I'm about to ad-lib a birds and the bees talk when Mae hands me a sheet of questions to ask them: "What's your name? Where do you come from? How many people in your family? ..." The kids know all the answers, though speak them in a Dalek-like voice, which makes me think that they don't know what they're saying: "Name Pui. Four year old. Five people family. Exterminate, exterminate." Picture cards are then spread on the floor for a game of match the rhyming words. The rules are that I say a word that describes one of the images on the cards, and they have to pick up that card and also a card that depicts a word that rhymes with the word I said. They go nuts for it — so much so that I decide I'll sell the format to the BBC for a million pounds for use on Saturday night TV. Mae then plays some videos so the kids can sing and dance. She says, "Come on, Mark, we have to show them what to do. You sing, and I'll dance. Three, two, one ..." I live out my rockstar dreams, singing — Sex-Pistols-style — classics like *Heads, Shoulders, Knees, and Toes* and *I'm A Jelly Bear, I'm A Gummy Bear*. The class ends with me pointing at picture cards on a board and the children repeating the words after me. I test each of them on all fifteen images, which depict words ending in -*all*. When you say fall, ball, and tall fifty-plus times each, they stop sounding like real words, and you start to question both your sanity and whether the English language is little more than a frail fiction that could collapse at any moment. After the last kid has left and I've done a final check for puddles, I fall into a chair, utterly frazzled. No chance I could do that all day, every day. If I find myself with a child of my own, the little sod will be off to a Singaporean boarding school as soon as he can walk.

From here, I'll travel to the province of Maha Sarakham in the north of Thailand, 450 km from Chachoengsao. I'll go with Ben — someone else I worked with at the uni — and his Thai wife Pear to spend Songkran there. Songkran is the Thai New Year holiday; it lasts for five days and starts tomorrow, so we're expecting heavy traffic — like bank holiday traffic times five. Millions of Thais from the north work in and around Bangkok because of the paucity of decent work where they're from. In Bangkok, working in a factory or on a building site or in a 7-Eleven, they might earn £5 a day instead of £3 a day in a rural village sorting mangoes or planting rice. This is the one time a year they will go home to visit their family. And it's as bad as we feared, the traffic: We set off at 10.30 pm, and from the start, we're stagnant in paralysing congestion, where all that moves are motorcycles shooting in and out between the buses and cars, weaving insouciantly through the nightmare gridlock. Out the window, a flat, raggedy landscape, and here and there a small town; dark houses, petrol stations, 7-Elevens, car dealerships, and factories, dismally rolling by in slow motion. Thailand is beautiful, and it is also bleak.

Slow progress, depressing scenery, but at least I'm comfortable in an air-conditioned Ford Fiesta, not crammed cross-legged in the back of a pickup truck with a dozen or more others and bulky packages, as thousands around us are. Others are in lurid disco buses that pump bass and flash lights: through the windows, I see people getting smashed and dancing in the aisles. There's constant battling for position, and drivers annoyed at the insufferable progress take turns to recklessly charge up the hard shoulder. We see a couple of accidents within the first two hours — and also a truck smashed and overturned on the side of the road that seems to have been abandoned. Six hours in, we're at 160 km, and some drivers are desperate: with the hard shoulder now also at a standstill, some speed along the wrong side of the road — which has hardly any traffic — to gain some quick ground. A stream get caught out and have to be let back into our side when a bus comes the other way. An hour later, I see an upturned pickup truck, the driver's cabin flat. Dozens bound the scene, taking photos — "That will get me a few Likes." — as the dead and injured are removed on stretchers. I can't tell how many killed, but half the trucks we've seen had groups sat in the back; if that were one of that half, the casualty count might be ten, could be twenty.

The reckless driving in Thailand is unlike what I've seen

in any other country, and the horrendous accident stats are no surprise. I blame the police. I mean, the drivers, of course, they're doing the driving, driving like dickheads — and I've been in a minivan where the driver stunk of beer, and I've been in another at night when the driver fell asleep and we bounced off the central reservation — but they only drive like dickheads because it's known that the police will take a bribe if they catch them driving like a dickhead. Driving down the hard shoulder or the wrong side of the road, driving while drunk, driving 200 km/h — all can be paid off on the spot, and you can be off on your way again, driving 200 km/h down the wrong side of the road while swigging a beer.

If you're wealthy enough, you can even get away with killing someone; even get away with mowing down a cop. There was a big story in 2012 about a police officer on a motorcycle being hit by a speeding Ferrari; the car was travelling along Sukhumvit Road at 177 km/h and dragged the crushed body along the road for a hundred metres before it fled the scene. The police tracked down the car — there was a brake fluid trail from the scene of the accident to where the driver lived — and tests showed the driver was both drunk and high. He was charged with speeding, fleeing the scene of an accident, and reckless driving causing death. And then … nothing. He's been photoed on beaches, at parties; he's travelled abroad but is still mainly in Thailand — he's not on the run. No arrest warrant. No manhunt. Because the key fact in this case is the name of the bloke driving: Vorayuth Yoovidhya. A name that means nothing to anyone outside of Thailand, but that surname is known to all Thais. His grandfather, Chaleo Yoovidhya, invented Red Bull. Chaleo died a couple of years ago but was a billionaire; at the time of his death, he was the third-richest person in Thailand. You can pay off a lot of people with billions — even the attorney-general.

And it's not just for traffic offences that the police are like this. A girl who worked at a hostel I stayed at in Thailand before told me they had to pay the police every month. I asked what for, and she said to avoid problems; said that if they didn't pay, there would be "complaints" filed about noise or drugs or whatever they wanted to make up. She said they didn't have to pay much, like £75 a month, but they did have to pay. Once a month, a cop would come and collect an envelope with the cash. And this wasn't a party hostel: there wasn't any noise, and no one even smoked spliffs there. £75 a month from that hostel, and £75 a month from every other hostel and hotel. And £75 a month — or quite likely more — from each club and bar. That's a lot of £75s every month.

Plus there's money from people trafficking, smuggling narcotics ... Their grubby fingers are in all the pies.

The Thais know this, know that the police are corrupt. Even the kids know it. When I was teaching in Thailand, lots of boys wanted to be police. I asked why. "Money!" And they didn't mean the salary, which is similar to a teacher's salary — a few hundred pounds a month. What was extra interesting was that it was the naughtier children who wanted to be police: the dicks and dossers and wasters, not the do-what-they're-told nice kids.

No nation is uncorrupted, but this nation is unfucking-believably corrupted. The police are corrupt, as well as the judiciary, and so are the army and the politicians. In less than a century, the country has had a dozen-or-so coups — and half-a-dozen more that failed. I was here for one of them, in 2006. Thaksin Shinawatra, a billionaire businessman, had been voted into power as prime minister twice. In 2001, his Thai Rak Thai party won 40% of the votes, compared to 26% for the Democrat Party, who came second. For the 2005 election, he was up to 60% of the votes. Then came the 2006 army coup, and he was charged with corruption; he fled the country and has not been back since. The army had their man in for a year before the next election in 2007; that was won by Samak Sundaravej of the People's Power Party — a rebrand of Thaksin's party, which was forcibly dissolved. He lasted eight months before being booted out by the courts for having another job while being PM — he was hosting a couple of cookery shows: *Tasting and Grumbling* and *All Set For 6 am*. His successor, Somchai Wongsawat (a brother-in-law of Thaksin Shinawatra) lasted less than three months: After an eight-day siege of Bangkok's airports — that stranded hundreds of thousands of foreign travellers — the courts disbanded the governing party and kicked out the prime minister for "neglecting his duties" in another position he held eight years prior. With the opposition dissolved, the Democrat Party — favoured by the 1% of Thais that own 50% of the country's wealth — at last got their bloke in: Abhisit Vejjajiva, who was born in the UK and studied at Eton College with Boris Johnson. The next election in 2011, Yingluck Shinawatra — Thaksin's sister — won. Now Yingluck is being accused of corruption — and I'm sure she is corrupt, as all of the fuckers are corrupt — and the Democrat Party want an unelected "People's Council" to replace the democratically-elected government.

And then there's what's above politics, what in theory should be aside from it, but what is in truth pulling all of the strings in this country. And what is that?

I can't say.

I could, but I'd then be jailed if I ever return to Thailand: Like Harry Nicolaides, who was jailed in 2009 for writing one paragraph — 103 words — on this topic. He wrote those words in a 2005 self-published novel, *Verisimilitude*. Fifty copies printed. Seven sold. Yet three years later — Thais are very slow readers — they arrested the bloke. At court, handcuffed and wearing heavy, rusted shackles, they sentenced him to three years in jail. He was in a twelve-by-five metre cell with fifty other people, locked in there from 4 pm until 6 am each day. In that one-bog cell were rapists and murderers, as well as a Russian arms dealer — "the Merchant of Death" — and a Canadian paedo known as "Swirl Face".

Ampon Tangnoppakul, a grandfather in his sixties, wrote even less for his 2011 jailing, and his words didn't even make it into print. Four text messages sent to one person. Five years in prison for each of them, for a total of twenty years. Ampon didn't spend the whole twenty years in jail, but only because he died one year into his sentence.

It's a high price to pay for a few laughs for my seven readers, and I won't pay it. I'm too good-looking for jail.

MAHA SARAKHAM

We arrive at 10.30 am — a twelve-hour journey — at a half-dead hamlet in the middle of nowhere. It's old eternal Thailand; the tumbledown Thailand of vegetables, paddy fields, dirt roads, of pigs and chickens and buffaloes, of squat toilets, muddy rivers, and sticky rice. Much has changed in Thailand, but, in these parts, it's the same as it was. A vegetable economy a century ago; a vegetable economy today. They scratch a living from the land; the pay is poor, and terrible are the prospects. They mend their shoes, their clothes, their vehicles. They're schooled and aren't illiterate, but there are no libraries, no bookshops, so though they can read, they have no advantage over those who can't. Kill the imagination, and work hard in a field: that's the way to live here. But they're sheltered, clothed, fed — it could be worse.

Pear grew up here, and her Mum still lives here, in one of the huddle of houses — several wooden — at a crossroads that comprise the whole place. Locals greet us as we get out of the car; hugs and handshakes. One man shakes my hand, then grabs my balls with his other hand. He does the same to Ben, which makes me feel better because a sexual assault shared is a sexual assault halved. Cobwebs and dust fill every nook of Pear's family's house. Pear says her Mum is too old to clean the house properly — and, yeah, she is pretty ancient, so fair enough — and so Pear sets about cleaning it herself. Ben and I should help, but it's against Thai culture for men to do chores, and after an overnight road trip without sleep — a half-hour doze at best — I've not got the enthusiasm to champion the feminist cause. So we skulk off to drink Sang Som, a Thai spirit distilled from sugarcane.

Chicken is for lunch, but we first have to catch it. The dozens running around sense they're on the menu and flee. We set off in pursuit.

Me: "Get that one."

Ben: "Which one? They all look the same."

Me: "The fat one. It'll be slowest."

Pear's Uncle: "*Gaiiiiiiiiiiiiiiiiiiiiiii.*"

Me: "What did he say?"

Ben: "Chickeeeeeeeeeeeeeeeeen."

Me: "Fair enough. *Gaiiiiiiiiiiiiiiiiiiiiiii.*"

After dashing around fields for fifteen minutes, we finally corner and catch one. Held by the neck, it's taken into a shed. An hour later, it returns in grilled pieces, which we sit under the shade of a mango tree to eat.

A middle-aged woman — who's joined us for a chicken thigh — tells me via Pear's translation: "I have two beautiful daughter. You want marry? You handsome foreigner. You rich. I want them marry you. You can choose which one like best. One seventeen year old, one eighteen year old."

I need Pear to translate as my Thai is awful, even though I spent two years in the country teaching. I was lazy to learn the language — that I can't deny — but in my defence, this language is particularly troublesome. There are seventy-two characters in the Thai alphabet — all an illegible scribble, unlike, say, Malaysian, where the words are foreign, are gibberish, but the letters are Romanised, so you can have a good stab at how they're said. And Thai uses no spaces between words, nor even punctuation. When it comes to speaking, there are also five tones to deal with: low, high, middle, falling, rising. If you know a word but say it in the wrong tone, it can mean something completely different. For example, the word *ma* can mean four things — dog, horse, bite, come — with the meaning changing based on the tone. To say, "The dog came and bit the horse", you'd say, "*Ma ma ma ma.*" But you must subtly change the tone of *ma* each time. Get the tones confused, and you end up with: "Come and bite the horse, you dog."

I did pick up some words, like "hello" — but not "good-bye" — and numbers and several colours (red, blue, green, black, but nothing fancy like orange or purple), as well as rice, pork, beef, fried egg, and some random vocabulary such as "keys" and "ticklish" and "sit down". And with that in my locker, said in an accent that was somewhat Brummie, somewhat Chinese, somewhat French — picked up from classes at school — and an array of facial expressions and gesturing and pointing, I managed not to starve or die. I learnt that much can be said with few words, that it's not hard to get by in a place where you don't speak the language. I learnt that if you go to a restaurant, it's obvious that you want food. Whether you utter Urdu at them or garble your order in Greek, they'll bring you food of some sort. And that the same principle of obviousness applies to buses, hotels, barbers, everywhere. Dealing with details is a problem, but so long as you don't mind sleeping in a shed, eating donkey intestines, travelling to the wrong place, or having a hairdo like Krusty the Clown, you can get by.

After lunch — by which point Pear's uncle has been KO'd by too much Sang Som — we go to a lake to catch some fish. A homespun countryman attempts to teach me to use an oval-shaped fishing net. I hurl it into the lake as far and wide as I can — which turns out to be not very far and not very wide. I wait a minute, then wade into the water to gather the net and bring it back to the bank to tally my haul. After triple checking the numbers, my total number of fish is zero. Give me a fish, and you'll feed me for a day; give me a fishing net, and I'll starve. The man tries it a couple of times himself and also catches nothing, which I have mixed emotions about: I want to eat fish, but I don't want to be exposed as an incompetent fisherman. He goes away and comes back with a different style net, similar to those used for badminton. He and Ben each take an end of the net and stretch it out under the water, then plod up and down with it. It's not riveting viewing, so I challenge Pear and Ben's son to a mud-fight — which I lose. The blow of defeat is softened by seeing the others have caught a dozen fish.

I'm covered in sweat and mud. A shower would be refreshing, but there isn't one. There's no running water at the house, only a couple of containers of rainwater: one for drinking, one for washing. I use a bowl to scoop out water and pour it over myself. Then I take a dump. "Ben," I shout, couched above the hole, "the bog roll has run out; can you bring me some?"

He calls back: "That bowl you used to shower ..."

Later, we grill the fish and eat it sat on the driveway of Pear's family's house. A guy turns up with a bucket of locusts that he's collected from a field. He tips them into a pan and fries them alive; then he shares them around, getting some fish in return. Swapping locusts for fish is shrewd, and had he been dealt better cards in life, this man could have prospered on Wall Street. The fried locusts are crunchy on the outside, gooey on the inside. They don't taste too bad. Anything tastes okay if you fry it first and wash it down with alcohol.

As we eat, Pear talks about the people in the village: "People my family's village, many not have job, but some have land a little, so can farming. My family have land for farm rice. Normally it good, but now have problem with government about buy rice."

Ben explains that Thailand is the world's largest exporter of rice, and the Thai government sought to flex their power on the international market by hiking its price. But the fools didn't factor in that buyers might baulk at paying inflated prices when there are other rice-producing countries they could buy from. Which is what they did, leaving Thailand with an excess of rice. Instead of farmers getting more for their produce — as promised by the government — they're now struggling to sell it at all.

But despite that balls-up, people like these are fully on board with Yingluck — and Thaksin before her. These pinched backwaters — rural, northern, dismissed for decades — are who Thaksin targeted, as well as the general working class. He offered them farming subsidies and low-cost healthcare, a whole string of measures to alleviate poverty — and allegedly even paid them cash for their vote. He also swore that within sixty days, he'd sort the drugs issue — that at the time was raging in the country — and as an issue that affects the poor more than the rich, that too won him a lot of votes up north. And he was true to his word on drugs: 10,000 were swiftly arrested, and more than 2,000 alleged dealers were shot dead in the streets. Amnesty moaned. But my boss at school said it sorted the problem in that town. If you look at a map that shows seats won in the 2005 election, the top half of the country is almost all the red of Thaksin's Thai Rak Thai party. The lower half is all blue, not one win for the reds. It's Thailand's equator, its north-south divide. In the north, says the stereotype, they're dark-skinned, insect-scoffing hillbillies, are haven't-a-clue dipshits who should be treated like children. And in the south, if you ask a northerner, they're materialistic, privileged wankers, uncaring and stingy and aloof. Crude stereotypes, but not without a pinch of truth, and to know Thailand, you have to see the north, by which I mean north of Bangkok.

Old Thailand, of course, isn't a tourist destination, and many come to Thailand for the southern beaches alone: they luxuriate on the white sand and, at a push, visit a temple and an elephant sanctuary. All many tourists see is that; they don't see the rest, yet they say they've "done" Thailand — like it's a one-piece jigsaw. But Thailand is large and much more than its beaches, and if you don't see the top half of it – the rice fields, the farmers, the buffaloes — you'll know next to nothing of Thailand. Which is why, whether Thailand or anywhere, I think you have to see at least three places, spread geographically, so that you can compare and triangulate. Only then is a claim to have "done it" even vaguely credible. If I hear, "I went to Mexico; it was *amaaaaazing!*" my first thought is, Did they go to Mexico, or just to a resort in Mexico? Because for the majority, the posh hotel or resort is the destination, not the country. Mexico might be *amaaaaazing*, but such a person isn't the one to ask. Stay in a gated, guarded palace with a pool and an Italian restaurant and a tennis court, and even shitty Scotland will be *amaaaaazing*.

After we eat, it's time for a water fight. During Songkran — which comes at the hottest time of the year — Thailand turns into a water-fight battlefield. Everyone has the right to soak anyone. Super-Soakers are the standard weapon of choice, but some prefer the grenade-type approach of a bucket. In Ben's car — he's pretty pissed, but so are all the other drivers, so it's alright, right? — we drive around nearby villages, several of which are like mini-festivals: people playing guitar, singing, drinking, dancing; many wearing oversized bright shirts, on them birds or flowers or pineapples, rather like Hawaiian shirts. Lots line the roads: chucking water, swigging Sang Som, bopping to techno beats. I drive-by shoot some: poke my water gun out of a marginally wound down window and squirt them in the face. It's more fun than Christmas, which most spend cooped-up in their house watching shitty TV. For Songkran, you're outdoors in the sunshine, mixing with all and sundry.

After more Sang Som, I retire to my bed for the night: a mat in the corner of the living room. Roaches scurry across the floor; mosquitoes pester me. I'm too warm if I cover myself with a blanket for protection, but I get bitten if I don't cover myself. I look for a cupboard I could sleep in; they're all too small. I'm so tired that I fall asleep despite being feasted upon. But not for long: I'm woken by the sound of a crack from within my mouth. I look in the mirror and see a chunk of a front tooth veneer — which I had fitted in Bangkok — has come off. Shit. A dentist up here? Fuck that.

LAOS

VIENTIANE

I arrive at the Laos border via a through-the-night bus from Bangkok. Yes, Bangkok, not Maha Sarakham. I backtracked to Bangkok to get my tooth fixed. The dentists in these parts I didn't trust, and to spend the next months — until I reach Europe — resembling a broken-toothed hillbilly wasn't an option either.

I cross into Laos over the Mekong on the Friendship Bridge and pay £28 for a visa-on-arrival. Twenty minutes from the border, Vientiane is the largest city in Laos — which is like saying it's the tallest hobbit in The Shire. I call it Laos, but it's Lao PDR, actually; or to be very precise: The Lao People's Democratic Republic. And because it has "Democratic" in its wordy name, it's, of course, definitely not democratic. It's in a select group in the world, a group of only five. North Korea is one. Cuba is another. The others are Vietnam and China. In these five, the red flag, the sickle and hammer, remains flying. It's flown in Laos since 1975; since then, Laos has been a one-party socialist state. All parties but the communists are banned. A ballot paper here looks like this:

A) The Lao People's Revolutionary Party.

B) The Lao People's Revolutionary Party.

C) The Lao People's Revolutionary Party.

That, in part, explains Vientiane's stunted size. Though the capital, it has a population of only 700,000; that's 8% of Bangkok. It also explains why it's a capital without a McDonald's. Or — and after Thailand, this seems unfathomable — a 7-Eleven.

Drab, joyless: that's the cover. And also quite a lot of the chapters. It's a jumble of shabbiness, is scruffy and scarred; if it were a face, you'd know it would belong to a woman abused. A little make-up can't hide the past. It has ugly, grungy, concrete buildings, run-down and stained with mildew, and plenty of barred windows; has blocky, sinister ministries, and the National Institute of Fine Arts looks like a cross between a warehouse and a shed. Dogs roam, and flat-tyred cars are left to rust out front of shambly houses and once-grand-but-now-decrepit mansions crumbling. Half the traffic lights don't work, and across the city are knots of cables tangled, like in Bangkok; wild, black vines that stretch across streets and between buildings; some slung low enough to swing on. It has a mall, Lao's largest: the four-storey Talat Sao. From the front, it looks a vaguely futuristic Chinese temple — if you don't look too hard and have a creative imagination. Inside, it's tube-lit and dingy, anorexic and depressed. Sellers are stood idle and stopped escalators ascend to upper floors that are empty and dark.

But that's not the full tale, for it's a sort of exotic communism. It's communist, but it's also Buddhist, and also French. It has sunshine, for starters — and that always helps. It has tropical trees, from which reds and oranges bloom, and trees that sprout through pavements, offering shade; from them, birds sing. It has too a National Cultural Hall that's a gold and white ludicrous decoration, as well as plenty of gaudy temples with cartoony statues — almost Disneyish — and some colonial confection: villas now banks, hotels, restaurants, with tile-roofs and painted in pastels, as well as cafes and bakeries — croissants, baguettes, cheese, coffee, wine. It's not modern, but modern isn't all that. "Modernisation" is generally mindless aping of the West, and with that comes good, yes, but bad too. Here is organic, with few concessions to tourists dollars. And it's lazy, which is meant as a compliment. To be busy seems to be some sort of badge of honour, but who wants to be busy? I like it, and to live here wouldn't be a hassle.

The people, I also like. The government is communist, but the people are people. And are, anyway, Buddhists before they're communists. They exude a calmness, a courteousness. Even the tuk-tuk drivers are chilled. "Tuk-tuk?" That's the whole of the pitch, and a "No, thank you" is simply accepted. Then they subside to the slumber they partially woke from. No touts, nor sharks; from darkened doorways, no "Massage?" The only solicitation is from ladyboys lingering on corners.

I eat some grilled chicken with sticky rice, and I drink a coffee — local style; iced and milky and sugary — then I walk more streets, among wonky homes and the stinks of drains and the smells of cooking from tiny, filthy restaurants. Through doors open, I see into plain rooms of people ironing, sleeping, chatting, people living like you, like me, and see, at a market, chickens strangled and squealing swine in a truck. I see parasols and plastic stools and fold-out tables, diners eating bowls of noodles, fatty pork spring rolls, thick sausages charcoal cooked; and see a man on a motorbike, a stack of eggs on the back — six dozen or more — kept in place with one hand, while the other steers. I see women wearing conical wicker hats sell fresh produce — honeycomb, bamboo, ginger — and others that march about with poles over their shoulders, a heavy load of wares stored in dozens of buckets balanced on either end. One man sits beside a stack of chickens piled on top of each other, their feet tied together to prevent escape. Another bloke has adopted a specialist approach: selling what appears to be an elephant tusk. I don't know what use anyone would have for it — other than sticking it on their forehead and pretending to be a rhino, which would be fun for only a short time.

Next to Wat Si Muang, beside a statue of Sisavang Vong, I chill on a bench in the shade, when across to me shuffles a pensioner — five foot tall, wearing a faded Hawaiian shirt, using a blue piece of piping as a walking stick. We each smile, say hello. I ask where he's going. He says, "Sit here, with you." And next to me he sits. He tells me his name is Som. "I old man," he says. And he's right about that: he looks very, very old. When I ask how old, he says, "Seventy year old." Then he corrects himself: "No, eighty year old. Eighty." His English is stuttering, but I stitch pieces together. He says he lives nearby with his daughter. When I ask how many children he has, he says, "One daughter," then pauses and adds, "Six sons."

"Wow, seven children."

He nods, smiles, pauses. "Now only daughter left. Son die. All son die."

I think: What do I say to that? How is the obvious question, if a possible impolite one. "How?" I ask. "How did they die?"

He mumbles a while, and I don't catch anything except "Laos" and "Vietnam".

After a short silence, he says, "Soldier," and mimes shooting.

He mumbles some more, then says, "Thailand boxing. I don't like. Laos no boxing."

I don't know what that means. If he means actual boxing, or if he means politics or war. I ask, "You boxing?" — which doesn't really mean shit, but I'm just trying to stick to words he knows.

"No boxing," he says.

When I ask if he's ever been to Thailand, he laughs and says no. His laugh is almost a guffaw, as if I've asked if he's ever been to the North Pole, not a country a few hundred metres away.

More quiet, which I break with my go-to lines: "Laos is such a great country! ... The food, the people, wonderful! ..."

He smiles but doesn't reply.

Soon after, he says, "I old man," and walks back to where he came from.

Som, if he's eighty, would have been born in the 1930s. A lot of troubles in those years from then to now. Laos — along with Vietnam and Cambodia — was part of French Indochina from 1893 until the Japanese seized Laos in World War II, after which the French returned for a while but were booted out in 1954. Then came civil war, and while that was ongoing, the country became entangled in the Vietnam War, was a sideshow battlefield that the Americans bombed to fuck. That over, communists seized power. That's a whole load of shit, and ol' Som lived it all. All that boxing, that's how he lost six sons, and Som himself certainly would have fired shots and been shot at.

When I saw Som, my first instinct was an internal groan — he'll want cash. But not only did he not want money, but none of the locals have asked. The one person who did ask was a shaggy-looking Australian who accosted me in the street. "Mate," he said, "I've got no money. Can you give me £1 to buy a sandwich?"

"You've not even got £1?"

"Nah, mate. I was waiting for some money to get transferred, but it hasn't come through. So can I have £1?"

When I told him I'm not an on-demand sandwich funding service, he told me to go fuck myself.

I walk next to Avenue Lane Xang — an own-brand Champs-Elysee, a wide, straight boulevard with trees along its length, and a central reservation of hedges and flowers. At one end, within a stone's throw of each other: the poncy Palais Presidential — grey with white trimming, touches of gold; a sacred temple — Si Saket; the oldest in Vientiane — the bland Ministre De L'Information, from which flies the red and yellow of the hammer and sickle, and which olive-uniformed officers walk out and in; and beside that ministry a mansion ruined. At the other end, a kilometre away, is the city's postcard landmark: an Arc-De-Triomphe knock-off called Patuxai. It's a concrete archway, mainly grey, with some pinkish details — like lotus petals and Buddhist imagery — and an ornate pointy roof. It has a hint of Taj Mahal, is a bit of a queer castle turret, but is best summed up by a display plaque on its side that says it's a "... monster of concrete ..." I'm sure that came out of Google Translate wrong, but it's not far off the mark. At least they didn't waste their own cash on it. The US paid for it. Though what they thought they were paying for was to expand the airport. Laos duped the suckers. I enter it and climb upwards, up a concrete stairway that feels like ascending a multi-storey car park, and on the fourth to sixth floors are stalls selling trinkets, hammer-and-sickle merch, plastic shite, and fakes. And I wonder, for a second, if this is a sacred, national monument, or it's a crap mall. At the top, I scan the capital that's hardly a city, look at the low, drab, modest buildings, the hodgepodge skyline — old by new, tall by short, plain by fancy, residential by commercial. I can just pick out Pha That Luang: a 45m-high stupa painted — not made of — gold. A bit of the Buddha in there, they say; a breastbone, maybe a pube. I see too a second, smaller, stupa: That Dam — the Black Stupa — sits on a quiet roundabout, crumbling and weeded. It was once golden, say the locals, but they also say that a seven-headed snake, known as a naga, lives in it, so ...

Looking down, I see an oval-shaped fountain, its water brown and grimy; next to it is a plaque that I earlier saw: "Grant aid from the government and the people of P.R. China as a token of friendship and cooperation between P.R. China and the Lao P.D.R.". "Friendship and cooperation" translates to China's bitch, and Laos will soon be a Chinese satellite. Special economic zones (SEZs) are mushrooming in the country, funded by yuan. These aren't simply China-towns, but "zones" — cities, practically — that are China in all but name: the clocks run on Beijing time — an hour ahead of Laos — and Mandarin is the lingua franca. They bring in money, but not for Laotians — except the high-ranking politicians who signed away the land on which they sprout for ninety-nine years. Then there's the railway. Little Laos has never had a railway. So Daddy China says, "I'll build you a railway; a £4 billion, 414-kilometre railway through Laos that will link up with the Chinese railway network." And you might think: So very, very kind. But China's not doing it for the good of Laos; they want access to Thailand, to Malaysia, to Singapore; to sell to people there and to ship their goods from there across the world. You say: "Yeah, so what? Laos gets a free railway. Everyone's a winner." No, not exactly. The deal comes with a clause: China will own it until Laos pays off the debt for it — which they never will. And that debt is on top of all the other debt — China is already the largest creditor to Laos — and while money is owed, China is the boss. Which is the Chinese method these days and is far easier than military threats. Its One Belt One Road strategy, unveiled in 2013, is colonisation by "investment" — power stations, railways, mines, roads, dams, ports ... Make a country so in debt that they have to bow and suck its cock: that's the plan. It's loan sharking nationalised and isn't a new idea: John Adams, second president of the United States, said, "There are two ways to conquer and enslave a country: One is by the sword; the other is by debt."

Laos, though, is used to it; as the Poland of Asia, it's been sucking for centuries. The Thais, then the French, and then — even though supposedly independent — the Vietnamese. It was in effect a colony of Vietnam for a while, who had troops in the country and "advisors" in power — their right, they said, after organising and equipping the communist Pathet Lao, who could never have seized power in Laos without Vietnam backing them. And that's a point worth noting: The Lao people never chose this path. A small percentage chose it and were only able to enforce it because of the Vietnamese. In 1975 — the year the Pathet Lao took over — only 1% of the population were members of the commie party.

For a decade after 1975, the logic of profit was binned for austere socialism. Borders were shut; the bankers and businessmen, missionaries of materialism, barred. Even China was cut off by demand of the Vietnamese, who had a tiff with who you would expect to be their comrades. But Laos was retarded by communism — it was a teenager that couldn't tie its own shoelaces — and relied on Soviet aid to get by. The collapse of the Soviet Union in 1991 — bye, bye free money — meant a slight pivot: "We'll use a pinch of capitalism, BUT — and note the BUT! — only so we can be better communists." And then Laotians got pizzerias and Pepsi. It also led to some awkward phone calls ...

"Hey, Australia, this is Laos. How's it going?"

"Laos?! Where the hell have you been?! I haven't heard from you in ages."

"Yeah, sorry, been a bit busy; you know how it is."

"Still doing that communism thing?"

"Yeah, totally. Love it."

"And hanging out with the Soviet Union?"

"Nah, not seen them lately. They sort of, like, died."

"Oh, right, shame."

"Look, anyway, I was wondering, any chance you can lend me some cash?"

"I guess so. £20?"

"Yeah, £20, but also £21,999,980 as well?"

"What for?"

"A bridge."

"And you'll pay it back when?"

"Well, when I said lend me, what I meant was give me."

"But your communism, doesn't that mean you can't accept donations from capitalist pigs?"

"We, err, rewrote the small print, so now we can."

Australia paid for the bridge — it was that bridge I crossed to come here, the cheesily-named Friendship Bridge, which was built in 1994 and was the first bridge between Thailand and Laos.

As the day fades, I make my way to the river, where is a promenade and a pleasant park. Shuttlecocks are swatted, and there are panting joggers, and middle-aged women do aerobic exercises to techno tunes that blast from battered speakers. A man is here with an open parachute on his back; he runs up and down, trying to catch some wind. I'm not sure if he's testing it for holes or if he's landed in the wrong place and is trying to take off again.

Across the Mekong is the Thai town of Nong Khai — and Vientiane is more like there than Bangkok. If you really, really wanted a Big Mac, you could swim it — just a hundred metres — and there are no walls or fences. It looks the same as this side, and if you didn't know it was a border, there's nothing clear that it is. I stare and think for a while; think how different a life lived on this side to that side is. If you're born there, capitalism; born here, a hundred metres away, and it's communism. That side, to call the king a twat will land you in jail. This side, no king — none of that nonsense. It applies the world over, to be born on one side of the line or the other, but here the difference is stark, and the Mekong between the countries makes it feel more dramatic.

A few hundred years ago, it wasn't a border. What is now Laos and northeastern Thailand was then part of the Kingdom of Lan Xang. That lasted from 1353 to 1707 before it split, at which point today's Laos was three separate kingdoms — Luang Prabang, Vientiane, and Champasak — each with their own king. The last monarch of the Kingdom of Vientiane was Chao Anouvong, and there's a statue of him in this park: on an ornate plinth he stands; he wears a sarong and pointy slippers, and a hat that's spiked; he has a sword by his side, and an open hand outstretched towards Thailand — where he died in prison after annoying the Siamese, as the Thais were then. It was only in the late-1800s that the kingdoms were reunited, via the French — "This is now French Indochina!" — and in the last light of the day, as I sit by the river sipping Beerlao, I think about how countries and borders are fickle, and how people die for nations that not long after other people don't even know the name of. And I conclude that people are stupid — always have been, and will be.

As I'm sat here pondering the transience of countries and the stupidity of people, a woman on a bicycle rides up to me. "Pedicure?" she asks. "I see feet you. Not beautiful."

"Did you say pedicure?" I ask, thinking I must have misheard, as it would be odd for her to ask me that.

She points to the front basket of her bicycle, which is filled with pedicure paraphernalia. "I give pedicure. £1.50."

"Here? Now?"

"Yes."

My feet do look manky, and more so than usual, because yesterday the nail on my big toe fell off after slowly dying since I hit it on a rock on a path on Railay.

I tell her, "You can't polish a turd."

"I not understand. You want pedicure?"

"No, thank you."

The nail on my other big toe fell off a few years ago after I banged it playing football, and it's never properly recovered. With a pair of rank big toes, I'll never fulfil my dream of being a flip-flop model.

VIENTIANE TO LUANG PRABANG

The *songthaew* — a pickup-truck-cum-bus — to take me to the station to catch the bus to Luang Prabang should have been at my hotel at 7 am, but it arrives half an hour late. The driver, a fat, gruff bloke, comes into the hotel reception looking like for breakfast he's chewed a wasp.

"Luang Prabang?!" he snaps at me.

"Yeah."

"Hurry! Quick! Now!"

Non-native speakers sometimes sound blunt and rude when they speak English — and fair enough; tone and nuance are difficult to learn — but this bloke is just a dick. Which he confirms when we get to the station by trying to palm us off into a cramped minivan for the trip north — us being me and the other foreigners from the *songthaew*. Seven of the ten do what he says and squeeze into the minivan. Me and two others stand firm and say we're not taking a minivan when we paid for a VIP bus.

"No big bus! Take minivan! Quick! Now!"

Still we refuse.

"Take minivan, get there 5 pm! Take big bus, not go long time! Get Luang Prabang tomorrow!"

Still we refuse.

The minivan leaves without us. A minute later, we're pointed to a VIP bus ten metres from where we're stood.

I say VIP, and that's what it was called by the agent who I bought the ticket from, and even what it says on the ticket, but it's a dilapidated Chinese bus — the signs on board are in Chinese. VIP, luxury, premier — such words should never be trusted by a traveller. But it's not always outright deception; the bus, shit as it may be, might really be "first-class" in that country. "Bus" and "minivan", however, if they sell you the former but try to put you in the latter, that's a scam. They're nouns, not adjectives. And it's not, by the way, that I'm so precious that I can't handle minivans — I've ridden in plenty, for four, five, six hours, even as long as nine — but for this journey, a minivan would be rough. Google says it's 350 km and a seven-hour drive. But while Google might know who Alexander Fleming is, it doesn't know how crap the roads are in Laos. I bet you my right bollock that it takes twelve hours.

We set off, and I'm soon asleep, knackered as I was working until 4 am because the internet only moved out of first gear after everyone else went to bed. After an hour on the road, I wake to find us pulled over by some trees. I peer out the window, wondering what's up, and see the bus driver stood outside with his back to the trees; he catches my eye, and a smirk spreads across his face. I look about him, and he takes a small step to the side. I strain harder to see what's going on and realise he's stood there to cover a woman who's peeing. His grin widens, and he winks at me. I look away — but it's too late: he thinks he caught me trying to peep on her. I wasn't, though, honest.

On the road again — the road that's windy and bumpy — I'm again looking from the window, watching Laos roll by: red earth and green trees, lots of palms, lots of commie flags; dusty, flyblown, scraggly villages with clusters of wooden houses and shacks; balloon sellers and ice cream vendors, roadside diners with Pepsi signs, mechanics and noodle stands; little stores that sell fags and biscuits and tampons, with red, glass-fronted fridges with shelves of bottles of Beerlao and Fanta; school kids idling their way to class — others, three, or even four, to a motorbike; temples in verdant grounds with ornate gateways; muddy brown rivers, mangy dogs — flea-bitten, nipples hanging — *songthaews* and bicycles and tractors. From the scenes, you'd think we're on some random backroad, but this is Route 13, the main north-south highway — the busiest road in Laos. It has no markings, no barriers, and is just two lanes wide, and is full of potholes — craters even. There are plenty plodding alongside the road, and there are more motorcycles than cars — the latter too pricey for most. Trucks, there are a lot, thundering and swirling gritty dust as they haul their loads from China and to China.

We curve through bucolic countryside, then it's more wild, more trees, and hills start to roll, and then come karst ranges — green, jagged, towering, and dramatic, like something out of Lord of the Rings. At the foot of these ranges, and beside the Nam Song River, is the low-rise scruffy town of Vang Vieng, and there we break for a while. I was here before for a weekend, a few years ago; back then, it was nuts ...

The area is nature at its finest, is full of caves and lagoons, but that was just a bonus, a pleasant backdrop for debauchery. People came to go "tubing" — riding tractor-tyre inner tubes down the river. And to make the tubing more fun, they got totally blitzed for it. At ramshackle wooden bars that sprang up along the river, bars that pumped techno and trance, young 'uns in body paint and bikinis mooned and got their tits out as they binged on Beerlao and home-brew Lao-Lao (45%) and shroom shakes, and smoked opium and weed. The bars, to draw in clientele, built crude towers and zip-lines and swings and slides so that the fucked-up people could launch and somersault themselves into the river. When night came, they'd return to town and zone out in one of the cafes that showed *Friends* on repeat — all day, every day — as they toked more spliffs and ate "happy" pizzas. Then to a club until 4 am — free shots of Lao-Lao! — before a short sleep at a £3-a-night hostel. Then wake up and again go tubing.

Great fun.

Until, in 2011, 27 selfish people spoiled it for everyone else by dying. Diving headfirst into the rocky river — some did that. Others drowned. Then there were the overdoses. That was a bad year — and the number is probably higher, as the 27 were just the ones that died at Vang Vieng's little hospital and not those that were transferred to Vientiane to try to save them — but the deaths had been steadily stacking up for years. It got so bad that many locals stopped going to the river, too scared of the legion of ghosts that had settled there — the dead ravers and stoners in purgatory, phantoms mooning while doing shots of Lao-Lao. Throw in the thousands of injuries per year too — the broken necks and legs and the gashes and the like — and all the ones that tripped so hard they lost their mind, and the Laos government — under pressure internationally — had to stop the fun. So, late in 2012, it all shut down. All the fun stuff, anyway, and now that you can only enjoy the natural beauty of Vang Vieng and go rock climbing and kayaking and all that other outdoorsy bollocks, there's not much point to the place.

It went from a tranquil farming village to the capital of backpacker degeneracy to an ok-but-you-can-skip-it-if-you-want spot. Next — Vang Vieng 4.0 — will be the Chinese iteration. That train line — "Thanks, Daddy China." — one of its stations will be here, and it will bring millions of Chinese to Vang Vieng. Many millions. And while the Chinese will likely show their bums and tits less than the white degenerates — "Dan, ya cunt, look at me crack! Wahey!" — it's debatable whether they'll be better for the locals. Because the Chinese travel on group tours, and they keep to their own: The tour guide is Chinese. They stay at Chinese-owned hotels, and they dine at Chinese-owned restaurants. The money, it all goes back to China.

And if, as is likely, Vang Vieng is "awarded" the status of SEZ, then the locals will anyway be booted out. It could become Laos Vegas. Actually, Laos Vegas 2, because already there's one: The Golden Triangle SEZ. It sits in a remote corner of Laos, at a point where Thailand, Burma, and Laos share a border. Carved from the jungle in the mid-2000s, it's a lawless playground of casinos and hotels and bars, under the control — a 99-year lease — of Chinese "entrepreneur" Zhao Wei. Its centrepiece is the Kings Romans Casino, a palatial building with greek columns and classical statues, with ceilings covered in frescoes; where boutiques stock tiger skins and ivory, and where bear paw soup and tiger bone wine are on the menu. Those that visit are mostly Chinese, as are most of the employees — even the prostitutes. And bills are paid in yuan, not kip. It attracts those who want a good time, and also those businessmen who dabble in what's not 100% legal, those who trade drugs, wildlife, people. It's not Laos, and it's not China, so the laws of neither are applicable — at least, not in practice. What happens in Laos Vegas stays in Laos Vegas.

The Vang Vieng residents would just vote that down, you say; maybe protest — "Hell, no, we won't go, stick your tiger bones where the sun don't show!" But communism doesn't favour votes, and as for protests, ask all the protestors in prison about that. The government wants an SEZ, they'll have an SEZ. Just like they did with the railway. The Lao people weren't consulted for that — a huge piece of infrastructure through the spine of its land built and owned by a foreign power. There was no referendum. The government wanted the railway, they'll have the railway.

The bus pulls out of Vang Vieng, and we ride on under a

skyline dominated by the hulking, rugged karsts. Fields here, fertile farmland; rice-growing villages, buffaloes, shacks on stilts, mud. It's old Asia undiluted, a landscape undateable, and as I watch it slowly unfurl, I watch too the figures in the landscape, the baggy clothes and wide-brim hats, the sun hot upon them; bent backs working laboriously — ploughing, digging, hoeing — a spine-breaking routine, the same routine as their grandfathers' grandfather, and also the same toiling routine their grandchildren will adopt. These people, they are Laos: some of the 80% of the six million Laotians that live in rural villages and work the land.

Strung along the road, patchwork houses; their front doors just a few metres from my gaze. No glass in the windows; sickle-and-hammers flying. Some, though, a few rungs up the ladder: solid and coloured — blue, green, orange; verandas and carved doors, with pickups out front, shiny and new. I see caged cockerels and fish hung drying, stacks of firewood and yellow crates of Beerlao, gasoline in whisky bottles at DIY gas stations, dogs flicking away flies with their ears, and meats grilling on oil drums halved — chicken, goat, bat. Pigs and cows are loose, bananas and papayas growing, also mangoes and pineapples, and there are many dumb-faced big-horned buffaloes, and, at one point, an elephant crosses the road. At spots are little stupas, which in Laos act as headstones. Within are ashes; the ashes from the open-air cremation of the corpse. The body is burnt on a pyre, along with the person's belongings. The whole village comes to see. They eat and drink and gamble for three days, at a funeral that's more of a party, then the body is burnt.

After the town of Kasi, upwards we slowly travel, on a road still dusty and neglected, a road that barely disturbs the scenes through which it takes us, hugging the contours of mountainsides unrelentingly steep. We turn and turn, to rise and rise, up, up, up, high into a raw, green landscape. Precarious ledges edged, and there are no barriers between the abyss and us. The turns, and maybe the heights also, are too much for the old guy in a seat near to mine; he starts to vomit into a little plastic bag. The bag soon whiffs and the contents start to spill over the top.

Straggling, unkempt villages passed that are sad in their simplicity — remote people, remote lives. Hard-pressed peasants, but some at least have satellite dishes. Waifs wash roadside at communal water taps while babies are bathed in buckets; other babies slung on backs — here, there are no prams. Some men with shovels digging into rocky earth, and some idly sitting the hours away. Whether working or sitting, they smoke. Even the very poorest of the poor can buy fags priced at £0.30 a packet. And Lao-Lao at £1 a litre. The government on this point is wise: Communism without affordable alcohol and fags, it wouldn't have lasted a year. Deprive them of their freedom, of 7-Eleven, of hope, but deprive them of booze and smokes, and they will revolt. They smoke, and they play around on their phones. It seems they all have one; not iPhones, but cheapo Chinese smart-phones — their fingers and thumbs tap-dancing across the screens. It's seen as progress — access to the internet = the wonders of Wikipedia = they can educate themselves out of communism and poverty — but the truth is they're used like toys: Play games, update Facebook, watch music videos and porn ... Everyone has a phone, but no one is any better off for it. If anything, they inhibit progress; for most, they're a distraction from being productive.

About that, I don't intend to patronise; I don't mean to say that they're wasters blowing the chance of a better life — playing *Plants vs Zombies* when they could be reading Alexander Fleming's Wikipedia page. Rich indeed would that criticism be coming from me, coming from someone as unproductive as possible. Someone who, when he's not drifting around on buses, making ill-informed observations about the world, makes websites move up and down on Google. All these people in these villages, these people who can dig, farm, make things, who can build and mend and hunt, are more productive than I am. Fact is, I can't do much, like most who have been to uni. I read some books and passed some tests, but skills, real skills, skills the world needs, well, no, I don't have them. And neither do you if you're a banker or a salesman or a consultant, which are a sort of scheming rather than a useful skill. Me, you, many: we exaggerate the importance of what work we do: "Oh, great, you're a graphic designer. But can you eat a logo? No? Wear it? Sit on it? Do any-fucking-thing with it? No? Yeah, I know, it's a cool logo, very cool, but the world doesn't really need cool logos. No, not even very cool logos." We get away with it for now as, at this point in history, the planet is alright and the people at peace. But a 2:1 in Business Law from Bournemouth University — yeah, that's me — ain't worth shit when the icecaps melt or the Fourth Reich rises. Then, I, you, many, will be exposed for what we are: inept fools.

On the way down, progress is even slower than on the way up. Tight, blind bends, and increasingly precipitous mountain slopes. The brakes and tyres creak and screech under the pressure. We stop a couple of times, and the driver, with concern on his face, gets out to inspect the thinning tyre treads, crouching and rubbing his hands over them. At one point, he checks under the bus, laying on his back and poking things with a metal rod. After that, he has a cigarette, and we crack on like everything is dandy. The saying, If it ain't broke, don't fix it, shouldn't be applied to brakes and tyres — don't wait for them to break before you fix them. Later, we get stuck behind a gravelling truck, which is slowly reversing down the wet road adding much-needed traction. Our driver hasn't the patience to wait, so we overtake and push ahead on the slippy road. This is definitely dangerous: this bus, this road. Particularly this stretch now, but I've seen evidence through the journey: I saw a car in a ditch, totalled; and stray wheels and bumpers, shattered glass. But what to do about it? Walk? No. You take the risk if you want to travel. It might be *your* bus that's one of those that plunges into a ravine, but it might not be. And if it is *your* bus, *you* might be one of the two dozen killed, but you might not be. And if it is *my* bus, it is *me*, well, they'll burn me on a pyre, burn me along with my flip-flops and laptop, so at least my Dad won't be pissed about the £10,000 to post me back.

As it is, it's not my day to meet my maker, and we arrive at Luang Prabang at 5:30 pm. A nine-hour journey, not the twelve that I bet you. To claim your prize, send a self-addressed envelope to:

Mark Walters
Some-Shit Hostel
Somewhere Random

LUANG PRABANG

Drums thump sonorously before dawn, as a conga line of shoeless, solemn monks with shaven heads walks slowly and silently through the foggy streets of Luang Prabang, past sparse-lit temples coloured golden and royal reds. As they walk, their bowls are filled by the hushed faithful, who sit, kneel, crouch at the side of the road, their heads lower than the monks' as a sign of respect; filled by women with long, black hair who wear ankle-length, straight, patterned skirts — the *sinh*, woven locally. Into the wicker basket that each saffron-robed monk holds are placed scoops of Laos's staple sticky rice; also biscuits and bananas. Every day here, in this moist, green valley bounded by peaks, starts this way, with this exotic vignette, this sacred ritual: the giving of alms; it has for as long as anyone can remember. At one point, at least a hundred stream by in single file along Sakkaline Road — that runs along the spine of this UNESCO-protected peninsula that's formed by the brown, murky Mekong and the still, green, Nam Khan River.

A place blessed by Buddha; a place that was once the capital of Lan Xang Hom Khao: The Land of a Million Elephants and the White Parasol. It could be a centuries-old watercolour: the monks, the Mekong, the mountains and temples and palms, the Indochinese shophouses, wooden homes, 1920s villas; and at its heart, the jungly Mount Phousi, crowned by a gilded stupa. If a place is delightful, normally people flock to it; and that crowd disfigures its beauty. But not here. Wars and communism, the terrible road to get here, the risk of rabies, malaria, dengue, Japanese encephalitis, have kept it out of touch and obscure. Westerners will never overrun Laos; its lack of beaches means it will not be the "new Thailand". Vietnam is more likely to rival that crown. The Chinese, though; that train line ...

Monks can't use money, so rely on this ceremony to get their grub. Locals give it to get some karma points; the more a person racks up, the better the life they'll have when they're reborn. Accumulate too few points and life as a dung beetle awaits. The monks are from the town's many temples — there are a lot; 30-odd. Why so many? Because the town was once a loose collection of villages, and each had its own temple. The temples are living, breathing institutions that perpetuate the sanctity of Luang Prabang; not attractions or museums. They aren't grand; small, in fact, like scaled-down models of those in Thailand. But bigger need not be better. The details are exquisite: Their doors carved and wooden. Gracious, sloping, curved roofs that rise to a peak. Their outers patterned with stencils and mosaics of lotuses and Buddha, with murals of the past. Their inners dark and cool; red carpeted, pillared, sparse; a front shrine of a dozen statues, shining golden. In the shady grounds: flowers, shrines, stupas, lawns, drums, bells; rooms to sleep, for eating — because these are not only places of worship; they are like little resorts, really, oasis for the mind.

I visit Wat Xieng Thong: an ornate, gilded temple; officially Luang Prabang's finest one. Ancient, twisted trees in the courtyard; bright butterflies and sprightly birds; bongs and chimes sound; doodle-doos. Monks gardening, sweeping leaves, doing odd jobs. They're young, mid-twenties on average. Lots have hairless bollocks to match their heads; mere boys that haven't grown pubes. They live for free in a scenic setting under sunny skies, away from the noise and clutter of the 21st Century, away from the world of profits and productivity; the world where the pursuit of pleasure is prioritised. A simple, languid existence, blissfully lived. To prevent pleasure luring them to Mara, women are to cover in the temples, no short skirts or vests: the last thing, they must think, a monk on the verge of enlightenment needs is the sight of a shoulder or thigh to send him back and horny into reality and despair ...

"Yes, ajarn, I believe I understand, understand all that you've taught me over the years, and that I now see the light, see ... a ..."

"What's that, my apprentice? You were saying?"

"Oh, err, sorry, it's just that over there, I see ..."

"See?"

"Erm ... "

"The light?"

"No. It's a ... a ...."

"Sure it's not the light, the light leading you to Nirvana?"

"Shut the fuck up about the light. A thigh, okay, I see a thigh, a woman's thigh!"

"So?"

"So?! I've got a huge boner. The light ain't nothing to a thigh. Man, I need a wank."

"But your training? Your decade of learning? You'll throw it away for a thigh and a wank?"

"Yep, see ya."

Something about Buddhism is tempting to me. It's a sweet sales pitch: to take one day at a time, to be cured of seeking pleasure. And I'm very much onside with the notion that if you can learn to be happy with less, it saves the stresses and headaches of striving for more. Many are the recipes for happiness, and maybe being a monk is mine?

I hear you scoff — "*You* a monk?! Har!" — but it's not as hard as it looks. The ones here, the ones in Bangkok, aren't meditating all day; they're out and about, walking around, and I've seen one in this town eating an ice cream and another practicing his keepy-uppy skills. In Bangkok, I saw them riding the Skytrain — which is not only free for them but seats are reserved for their pious bums — and in the 7-Elevens buying top-up credit for their phones. I didn't see any at Nana Plaza, but that's not to say for sure there weren't any there too. Because they do get up to mischief; now and then, it's on the news: all sorts of tales of monks behaving badly, stories of sex, scams, scandals, the Sangha sinning: a monk with his pants down, or one selling the kidneys of children, or embezzling the fundraiser for a hospital, or dressed up as a woman, or strung out on meth. There was a big story a year ago about a Thai one hiring a private plane to take him to Paris. He was snapped on the plane with his Louis Vuitton baggage. That caused uproar, and when he was looked at closer, it was found he had millions of pounds hidden away. One of the 227 official precepts — which are monk laws — is that they shouldn't even *touch* money but lots of them do and some of them are touching shedloads of it: I don't know about Laos ones but Thai temples collectively accumulate a few billion pounds every year. Billions! A lot of that is donated, but it also comes from blessings (new cars, new houses, new businesses, new children ...) and because Laotians and Thais are very, very scared of ghosts, from exorcisms. What do these supposed guardians of a country's moral soul do with all that money? Apart from buying golden Buddhas and Louis Vuitton baggage and first-class bus tickets, I don't know.

So a little misbehaving is overlooked. And for all the talk of their strict diet — one meal a day — half of them are overweight. As for all their worldly belongings in a single bag? Think these days how much you can fit in your palm, never mind a bag. An entire encyclopaedia. A thousand movies. A million songs. It's not like the old days, when they'd have to pick just half a dozen of their favourites: "I'll take *Buddhism For Dummies*, a VHS of *Big Wet Asses #12*, the Bee Gees's *Saturday Night Fever* ..."

Is it then that difficult?

Maybe not. And I'm already halfway there. I own hardly anything, am virtually possessionless. What I have in my one bag now, all I've had since Sydney, and all I'll have until Europe, that's all I need. My bag, so small, helps me focus on what I really need. It's an antidote to materialism. As for the same outfit day in, day out, well, I've worn the same jeans every day since KL. Orange, though, isn't my colour. It would be a deal-breaker. I'd insist on blue, which compliments my eyes.

I walk the town, the town of two-storey buildings, of browns and greens and white; I walk its alleys and lanes, and I sit in the shade, let it leak into my soul: Spirit houses and noodle stalls. Shophouses painted yellows, greens, blues; geckos on the ceilings, pictures of Buddha hung. Sheds and shacks with veg plots and chickens on the shaggy riverbank. Moored canoes, and canoes crossing, puttering across the Mekong. On the far side of the river: green; here or there, the odd roof or plume of smoke. Stilt houses that tumble into the water. Laotian music, its tones sweet and feminine. The locals say, "*Sabaidee.*" They say, "*Bor pen yang.*" A passing monk says, "Hey, yo, wassup?" Radios play and karaoke ballads are sung. Laughs and squeals from children. Birdsong. At lots of spots, simply drowsy silence. Corn grilled. Fish salted and cooked over coals. Trees with coconuts, with tamarinds. Bicycles. Wooden bungalows; mansions with balconies. Aproned grannies roasting bananas. Kerbside barbecues and steaming broths. A few fancy places where the whites are starched and in the glasses are wine. Weathered buildings — some spruced, some ruined — with dates engraved above the doors: 1951, 1934, 1927. Echoes of the French: Parisian-style cafes — Le Banneton, Cafe Ban Vat Sene; pâtés and pastries and baguettes. The Ecole Primarie — faded yellow, roof tiles falling — its doors and shutters opened, the kids inside chanting. By the Nam Khan, bananas growing and flowering trees; nude boys play — they somersault, splash, show off. Tuk-Tuks ferrying backpackers to waterfalls; other backpackers cautiously crossing bamboo bridges. *Songthaew* drivers on a bench, doing shots of Lao-Lao; weed sold by some — they toke a pretend spliff to let you know.

On the lanes by Wat Mai, just off Sisavangvong Road, — a market. Women from the hills and the villages come to sell; food, mainly: Ten types of chillis; more of mushrooms. Garlic and ginger and honeycomb. Chicken kidneys, hearts, and livers on grills. Fish stuffed with lemon grass. Frogs skewered, catfish and toads and eels. Skinned moles — or are they rats? — and feathered birds. Tails, skins, organs, and bones. Fish the size of kids. Bowls of beetles, of snails. Bark and leaves and stalks and roots. Parts of pigs: ribs and chops and trotters. Buffalo brains — grey, shrivelled-up matter, floating in a bowl. Sticky rice and spring rolls and suspicious sausages. Some of it's vile, and there are sights to neuter your appetite. But Laos is poor and mountainous: They eat what they can. The guts, the skins, the brains, of all manner of creatures great and small — they consume everything, casting nothing away. It's easy to be sniffy, superior, about what they pollute their plates with, but what about us? Ask yourself: What's cheese? (Curdled milk.) And what's milk? (Liquid secreted by the mammary glands of cows.) As for KFC and Pepsi and pork pies ... Objectively, almost everything except vegetables, fruits, and nuts are vile. Still, I'm not eating a filthy toad.

I come out in a clearing beside a house on the riverfront, and an old fella approaches from a boat on the bank; he asks, "*Est-ce que tu parles français?*"

Another that thinks I'm fucking French. I say, "*Je m'appelle Mark. J'ai douze ans.*"

"*Tu as douze ans?*"

"I'm not twelve years old now, no, but I was when I learnt French at school. That's pretty much all I can remember."

"I speak French good. English just bit."

"Is that your boat?"

"Yes. Also, that one. And that one too."

"And this is your house?"

"This house number four."

"Where are the other three?"

"One over there. Two in the town."

"Cool."

"You buy me beer?"

"No."

A man with three boats and four houses can buy his own beer.

Someone else I spoke with also acquired something of a property empire. I'll be a bit vague as the guy was open with me — and didn't know I'd write it here — but the government wouldn't be happy with what he said, and if they knew who told me he'd be in the shit. The guy has a few ventures and properties in Vientiane. Yet he also still has a civil service position. "Why the job?" I asked him. Surely, I thought, the pay is crap and he could do without the hassle if he didn't need the salary. "To stay in the party," he told me. "You can only be a member of the communist party if you also work for the government." He told me he's low-ranking in the party but few rungs up from the bottom. He said he doesn't believe in communism but it's better to be in the party than not in it. "Especially if you have money, it's safer to be in the party. Then government officials and the police don't interfere with you."

"Interfere?"

"Ask for money, basically. They don't ask for it directly, but they create problems that only go away once you give them an envelope." He added, "They interfere less, anyway. It, of course, depends how high up they are; the high up people can still cause problems for the people lower down, even if they're in the party."

I asked how he got into the party to start with, and he said he first had to get a job within the government — which could be the army, the police, a teacher, a bureaucrat; that sort of thing — and then he had to be invited to join the party and be given the okay by other party members — literally the same way someone would join a golf club. He had to be a lackey for the person who had invited him, doing hours and hours of admin and paperwork for him for a few years, all for free. "It's like a test," he said, "so they can see you're committed and can be trusted with the inner workings of the party; to see if you'll keep the secrets and not let the normal people know it's all really a scam."

"And it is a scam, is it?"

"Of course. No one — well, almost no one — really believes in communism, in Marx and Lenin and whoever. In the official meetings, everyone pretends they do; we say the right things, we nod and agree and smile. But it's all for show. It's really about money."

"And power too?"

"Power is just a way to get more money."

As the sky turns rusty orange, and the sun slinks behind the mountains, a hundred stalls set up, and "You want shake? Sandwich?" is the call of the locals. Coconuts and pancakes are favourites with backpackers; as is an alley where you can fill your plate with as much food as you can fit on it for £1. They eat cheap food and they drink cheap whisky. "Let's go to Utopia!" they say. And: "Yeah, then let's go bowling!" People sell vests, shawls, dresses, bracelets, cushion covers, carved elephants, bamboo straws ... Junk mostly, handicrafts and souvenirs; no treasures from attics. You might think isolation and communism has made the locals naive about pricing and bargaining but that's not the case. It's the tourists that are naive: confusing the notes — "Is that 1,000 or 10,000?" — and swallowing stories of "locally-made" (all this crap comes from China). The locals hardly budge from their prices; they come down a little but only because the prices are inflated to start with. On this far-off bend of the Mekong, bargains are few.

Locals eager to practice English linger around the market: "Excuse me ..." Two lads speak to me. They're about eighteen. They're studying hospitality and are at the moment working in one of the town's fancy hotels for experience. "I want to work in Shanghai!" says one, his eyes bright with innocence. The other says: "Seoul! I want to go to Seoul!" I tell him I lived in South Korea. I lived in Sokcho, which is by the sea, a few hours drive from Seoul, but I went to the capital quite a lot. The lad says, "Tell me: How is Seoul? Is it amazing?"

"It's big, it's busy, it's bright. You know Bangkok ..."

"No, I've never been to Bangkok."

"Ok; you know Vientiane ..." And I plan to say it's, like, ten times bigger and better than that.

"I've not been there."

"Vientiane? You've never been to Vientiane? The capital of Laos." I try to be clear in case he thinks I said Vietnam.

"Vientiane I've never been to."

I ask his friend. He's also never been to Vientiane. The biggest, busiest place they've been to is here: Luang Prabang — population: 50,000. And I think: How can you explain cities like Seoul and Shanghai to people who have never been to any city. The scale, the sharks, the frenzy, the millions of strangers, the feverish confusion; you can't convey that with only Luang Prabang as a reference. Seoul and Shanghai are hundreds of times the size of here; the brain can't compute that. These boys, these sweet, kindly boys, I don't think they'd hack it; they'd drown in cities like that. But maybe they're anyway dreaming — fantasy is all it is. After all, their English is just ok, and they can't speak Korean or Chinese. So, I let them dream: "You'll like Seoul, like Shanghai — they're amazing. The girls have huge breasts and they love Lao guys. They love Lao guys a lot."

"Really, mister, really?"

"Yep. Really."

On the way back to my room, I stop off to buy a £35 bus

ticket to take me to Kunming in China, a 24-hour drive away. The prospect of that torturous journey is worsened when, at my room, I read an article on the BBC News website about a terrorist attack earlier today at the train station in Urumqi, the capital of Xinjiang.

"Deadly Terrorist Attack At Xinjiang Railway Station: A bomb and knife attack at a railway station in China's western Xinjiang region has killed three and injured seventy-nine others. The attackers used knives to stab people and detonated explosives."

A link is within the article to another one about a terrorist attack last month at Kunming railway station. But there's no point stressing about getting stabbed or blown up until I'm in the country, which isn't a certainty. That Mongolian visa the Chinese embassy told me to get, the one I didn't get, it's a valid reason to refuse me entry at the Laos-China border. I hope they won't give a toss. If they *do* give a toss, I'll see what the bribe is to make them not give a toss.

LUANG PRABANG TO BOTEN

Most "travel" is travel by numbers, is colouring within the lines. Real travel, conversely, is rather like art; is uncertain, unpredictable: It might turn out great or it may be shite. My today is uncertain and unpredictable. I know which direction I'm going — north. That's all I can be sure about today. I don't know how long it will take to get to the border. I don't know what will happen at the border. Will I tonight sleep in Laos or China? I don't know. I can't even be sure I'll make it to the border, as the bus I'm on is shit.

The bus is older than I am. It's a full-on sleeper: all beds, no seats. There are three rows of bunk beds, the length of the bus. I'm 178cm — an average height — but the bed is short for me; my feet poke over the end. The bed isn't short for the majority on board, as the majority on board are Chinese — including the driver. The other passengers smoke and gob — in the bus, not out the window. Blasting out of a fuzzy TV, a Chinese cabaret show. The suspension is a shambles; potholes are plentiful. I bounce like a kid with ADHD who's scoffed a bucketload of Skittles. I could have avoided all this: A flight would have cost about £100 and taken less than two hours.

The road is again Route 13 — the main north-south highway. Now even further from the capital, the road is in even worse condition than before. Long stretches are unpaved, simply gravel and damp mud. At one point, we pause while despondent workers in front try to even out the road surface — a battle they'll lose. Sinuously, tiredly, we crawl up and down mist-covered mountains; all steep slopes and foliage, shaggy wilderness; dramatic gorges and green peaks and ledges and cliffs. Series of sheds along the road at times — homes for families of unfortunates. Broken bricks hold bits of plastic over roofs; tin shack toilets. Now and then, precarious villages, shabby and shanty-like; not on a map, with no temple, no school, no hospital. The towns there are, utterly dismal; but still worth seeing: As Thoreau said, "It's not worth the while to go around the world to count the cats in Zanzibar." No, go around the world to see other people; see where they live, what they eat, etc. The temples, the elephants, the mountains — all that is dessert; it's not worth the journey simply for that. See the bad as well as the good; only then can you know the world.

I see one man stood alone by a wooden shack; he wears a nineties Chelsea shirt and has what appears to be a home-made prosthetic stump. Our eyes lock for a second, and I imagine a thousand things about him — what he thinks, what he longs for; what he loves and what he hates — and I wonder what he thinks of me, if he thinks what most other people think: that I'm a twat. Then away I go, and we pass out of each other's life. But, for a while longer, I think of him, of what must be a hard life up here — hard even without that pirate leg. Life's largest problems are universal — unrequited love, sickness and death (your own and others), bills to pay but not enough money to pay them, your partner cheating, friends letting you down, your phone screen cracking — but he has those and then some: A bad leg. A shit house. Grafting for a couple of quid a day — and no pension nor month of vacation nor promotion opportunities. "Life's so unfair!" is said when looking up at the people with more. Travel makes you look down at the many with less. Not just a passing glance — a bloke begging, a scruffy fuck on a bus — but hour after hour. At home, it can be ignored — the hobo asleep on the pavement. But for hour after hour? No. Especially when you're on a bus and poor is the only channel the window shows. And it makes me think, Yeah, life's so unfair, and it's unfair in my favour.

And that bloke knows it. Not so long ago, he didn't; not really, anyway. He may have been aware vaguely, but with no TV and no internet and no backpackers passing by, what was not Laos was just tales. For all he knew about other places, the UK or US may as well have been the moon. He didn't know, had no way of knowing, what London or New York were like. The moon, actually, he knew better: at least he'd seen that. Then came the internet, and came Google and YouTube. Now he knows. If you don't know better is available, where you are and what you do seems fine, and you can be happy with that — ignorance can indeed be bliss — but once you know, then what?

I wonder: What if I somehow offered that guy a shot at the UK? Arranged a visa, paid for his ticket. Would he uproot from his village that's all he's ever known? Here are his family, his friends, his memories. Would he leave it all behind for an unknown future in a place that he wouldn't understand, where he wouldn't be understood?

"Phet, the UK: fancy it?"

"Yes! It's my dream. Skyscrapers and theatres and black cabs, tea with the Queen, watching Lampard score at The Bridge, and living in Notting Hill with Hugh Grant as a neighbour. Sign me up."

"It won't be quite like that."

"What do you mean?"

"London, for a start; you won't be able to afford to live there. You'll have to live a little outside of London. A bit more north, where it's cheaper."

"Watford?"

"A bit more north than that. Maybe Carlisle."

"Oh. Well, at least I'll be rich."

"Bad news, my friend: you'll be poor. At best, you'll get a job as a cleaner, as a labourer, perhaps in retail. Minimum wage it will be: £6.50 an hour."

"£6.50! An hour! That's more than I earn in days now. I can buy a BMW and cocaine and hookers."

"But taxes, national insurance ... And rent will suck up a lot of it."

"Rent? I won't own my house like I do here?"

"You'll *never* own a house in England. Not even in a shit-hole like Carlisle. They cost over £100,000, and the banks will never grant you a mortgage, what with you being a toilet cleaner or warehouse monkey."

"If I rent, what sort of house will I get?"

"You mean what sort of *room*? You'll only earn enough for a room."

"Room? But I can't fit all my family in a room."

"Your family, they can't come."

"My goat? My chickens?"

"Sorry, no."

"That sucks. But, I guess, I'll make friends there."

"Not likely. You can't speak English, and also the locals kind of dislike immigrants. We put them on the front of newspapers and call them scum."

"It doesn't sound so great. I mean, I'd lose a lot of the good stuff I have here, and I don't really see what the upside is."

"It's not all bad. The pubs are good, and, err, yeah, the pubs. Oh, and lots of nice crisps that other places don't have: pickled onion, prawn cocktail, Worcester sauce ..."

"The pubs stock Beerlao?"

"No. We drink Carling."

"Carling? It's better than Beerlao?"

"It's kind of weak and pissy."

"I'll stay here."

And I think most would; most would stay here. Or maybe leave, then soon come back — even if back is a dirt floor shared with chickens and dogs, a hard bed to lie on, an open fire, and outside their door a litter of junk and a road noisy and muddy and traversed through the night and day by heavy trucks. Why? Because the majority of people stray not. Where they're born is where they live. They're tied to "home" at first by birth and later by the fear of living else-where. And it's maybe not so bad here. They have their Lao-

Lao, their nature, their community, and a lot of time to enjoy those things. I see them smile, watch them laugh; they're no less happy than people in Birmingham, and I know from my time living in Thailand that people there were also at least as happy as people elsewhere, people to who life was more than fair to. It's not mutually exclusive to be happy and poor. People have been happy throughout history without many of the things we today consider essential for happiness — an ensuite and scented candles, a deluxe grilled cheese sandwich toaster ... Even they, who have seemingly nothing beyond basic, have more than 99.9% of the world had a century before now. They are better off than your great-grandfather.

We stop to let off a woman, and a French bloke — one of the three non-Chinese on board — gets off for a piss. While he's mid-piss, the driver closes the door and starts driving forward. The look of horror on the Frenchie: He runs after the bus with his still pissing penis in his hand, fearing he's about to be abandoned. He wasn't; the driver was just moving forward to let a truck pass. The roadside piss-stop is the only sort of piss-stop we've had — one every four-or-so hours. No service stations in these parts. If you need a dump, you take to the bushes beside the road. But to go too far into the bushes is risky; those pesky UXOs ...

UXOs: unexploded ordnance — i.e. bombs. There are lots in Laos: the world's most heavily-bombed country (per capita). Lives are shattered by bombs that still litter the Laotian countryside from a war that they were never fighting. That war was the Vietnam War, and it ended 40 years ago; but Laos still lives under its shadow. Someone in the country is injured or killed by UXO every fortnight. That's not a stat from the past; that's now. The victims? Not soldiers but farmers and children.

Over nine years — from 1964 to 1973 — the plus-sized burger-munchers dropped more tonnage of bombs on Laos than they dropped during all of World War II — more than on Japan and Germany combined. Over a quarter failed to detonate on impact; those are the UXO lying in wait in rice paddies and forests and rivers. Why would the fuckers do such a mean thing to little ol' Laos? The Ho Chi Minh Trail.

Hundreds of kilometres long, the trail was a network of tracks running from North Vietnam through Laos and Cambodia and ending in South Vietnam. It supplied Vietcong guerrillas fighting the US. Laos was neutral and had no say about the trail. The North Vietnamese stuck the trail on their land; then the US tried to bomb the trail off their land. Laos just picked its nose and waited for the bigger boys to fight it out.

In both Luang Prabang and Vientiane, I went to UXO centres. Primitive prosthetic legs hung from the ceiling, and beside potted plants were a medley of bombs and other tools of death. I saw, on the floor, a split-in-two cluster bomb; each half looked like a small canoe; each was filled with tennis-ball-sized-and-shaped "bombies" — in total, hundreds. A sign by that cluster bomb said: "The canister breaks open in mid-air and the submunitions (known as 'bombies' in the Lao PDR) are released — effectively carpet bombing an area the size of two or three soccer fields ... Around 30 percent of bombies fail to detonate on impact, leaving unexploded zombies scattered across a wide area. When disturbed, even decades later, they can explode, injuring or killing innocent civilians." The bombs at the centres were cleared from the wild. That clearance mission is done not with high-tech equipment but with metal detectors and trowels. To clear a 100 m² area can take up to ten days. A shit job that has to be done; and they have to do it themselves because the fucking yanks didn't come back to do it. They have now, at least, admitted the nine-year aerial bombardment. At the time, the US denied it; denied they were carpet bombing Laos. The US public didn't know — it wasn't on TV, was kept out of the papers. If asked about it, the US government — Eisenhower, then Kennedy, Johnson, Nixon — for twenty years just said, "War? What war?"

"The one in Laos."

"Never heard of it."

"The country? Or the war?"

"Is it hot in here, or is it just me?"

"You're avoiding the question."

"Question?"

"About the war in Laos."

"Zzzzzzzzz."

"Look, I know you're not asleep. You're pretending."

"Oh, sorry, dozed off for a moment."

"Why won't you admit it?"

"Ok, I admit I was only pretending to be asleep."

"No, admit the war in Laos."

"Zzzzzzzzz."

There was a room at the centre in Luang Prabang that showed a movie that included translated interviews with Laotians maimed by UXO: A farmer lost his hand. He still farms — pretty inefficiently — because what else can he do? And there was a small boy: Digging for worms to fish, he set off an unseen explosive. He lost his eye. He said, "Before I always used to win at marbles, but now I lose." One girl built a fire to cook dinner, and the heat made a UXO underground detonate; now she has no legs.

To be disabled in Laos isn't the same as being disabled in Europe or the US; it's much, much worse ... No big payouts; no, "Sorry about that; here's a million dollars for the inconvenience of our negligence in blowing your hand off." And the healthcare system isn't free, as it is in, say, the UK; no NHS to patch you up and sort you out with a zippy motorised wheelchair. If a bomb takes off your limb in Laos, you pay for a shitty prosthetic or you make your own shitty prosthetic. If your testicles are blown to pieces, a doctor hands you a couple of ping-pong balls and a bill.

Since the end of the war in 1973, more than twenty thousand in Laos have been killed or maimed by UXOs. Of those, thirteen thousand lost a limb. How many died in 9/11 by comparison? 2,996. 9/11 got quite a lot of press; what happened here, as good as none. Most Americans couldn't even place Laos on a map — "Bro, is that, like ..."

We ride bumpily on through rubber plantations and forests, passing shacks on stilts lived in by locals in bright clothes — tribespeople of the north — and at 5.15 pm we reach Boten on the Laos-China border. Twenty years ago, this was a sleepy village of farmers. A few years ago, it was Golden Boten City. Now, it's vacant, an apocalyptic, desolate ghost town: Strips of shuttered shopfronts and deserted market stalls. Giant hotels forlorn and derelict — oranges, yellows, pinks; the paint peeling and blistering. Faded signage — all in Chinese. Car parks empty. Weeds. A handful of deluded shopkeepers — Chinese — remain; the only one I see with a customer is a market stall of porn DVDs. The abrupt change from village to boomtown came in 2003: A Chinese businessman, a 99-year lease, an SEZ. The developer's brochure for Golden Boten City depicted luxurious apartments, picturesque lakes, a golf course ... A casino, though, came first; discos, karaoke, brothels followed. Neon lights beamed as cashed-up Chinese poured in to party and play slots and poker, blackjack and baccarat — none of which they could legally do in China. The time, the money, the language: Chinese. About the only thing that wasn't Chinese were ladyboys imported from Thailand for a cabaret show. The Laotian customs office was edged a few miles south, meaning the Chinese coming didn't need a visa. They'd left China but hadn't entered Laos. It was thus a lawless no-man's land. It got out of hand, of course: kidnappings and ransoms; corpses in the river. Those who built up debts were imprisoned and tortured until relatives paid up. Big winners "disappeared". Drugs and crime rampant, newspapers stories piling up along with bodies, it had to end after less than a decade. The PR, the optics, were just too bad for the Chinese government who must appear to be running a tight ship in order to keep their billion plebs in line. China didn't officially shutter the city, but its Ministry of Foreign Affairs did as good as that by cutting off Boten's electricity. A call made, a switch flicked, and that was that: The end of Golden Boten City — the quarter of a billion dollars spent on it in the bin. New plans are afoot, though ... Here will be the start of the railway through Laos; a city of 300,000 is being touted; this time, no casinos.

We all get off the bus and walk to an empty-looking building. After eleven hours laid down on that bus — that sticky, stinky, smoky bus — my level of dishevelment puts me so far into scarecrow territory that I can no longer see the border with dignity. I fix up my hair a little, and I sprayed on aftershave before I got off the bus; I'm not sure why: I don't think the border guard will sniff me and let that sway his decision.

I'm more anxious than I thought I would be; dry-mouthed and sweaty as I line up in the queue — comprised of people from only our bus; ours is the only bus in the city. I don't have that Mongolian visa. I don't have a ticket — plane or otherwise — to take me out of China. But it will be fine, right? *Right?!* I mean, they think I want to stay in China forever? And do what?!

Two guys in olive-coloured uniforms at the entrance to the building search bags. They're friendly, they smile; it's a good sign. Then on to the immigration official: He flicks through my passport, searching for my Chinese visa; he finds it, then stamps me in. And that's it: I exit the building into China; no questions asked. My worries were unnecessary — as is typically the case in travel, and, really, in life.

To arrive like a spectre at the ragged fringe of China at dusk, after a journey through mountainous northern Laos, banged about on a crowded, beat-up bus: this is real travel. Not at the airport in a brightly-lit metropolis but surreptitiously stealing in via the busted back door; this is art. Now onwards to Kunming, to Kazakhstan via Xinjiang. It will be fine, right? *Right?!*

CHINA

KUNMING TO CHENGDU

I arrive in chilly, overcast Kunming after twenty-six hours on the bus. As I walk the streets, I get more than a few stares and double-takes. It could be because I'm a foreigner, or it could be because I'm walking around in flip-flops and a bright, striped jumper. The locals seem to have come to a consensus only to wear grey, black, brown clothing. From a food cart, I buy a pot of roast potatoes coated in spicy herbs. I hovered to see what others were paying, then blurted my best *ni hao* (Chinese for hello) and pointed at what I wanted. The seller asked me something, to which I replied with a nod despite having no idea what the question was. I thought this better than saying, "Sorry, I don't understand." Speaking in your own language — even a few words — is a mistake; it results in an exchange that sounds like one between a Furby and Siri.

Not a word of English anywhere. I should learn more Chinese, but it's tough. It took me an hour to learn *ni hao*. The language is comprised of thousands of intricate symbols. You need to know at least 2,500 of them to be able to read a newspaper. Unfortunately, the symbols don't depict the words. The symbol for *cat* isn't a small image of a cat — which would simplify learning the language. Another complication is there being several regional languages in addition to Mandarin (the official language). People use their regional language for everyday communication, and each of those is unintelligible to speakers of the others. But despite the regional differences and multitude of symbols, the consensus of international language experts is that English — with its subtleties, inconsistencies, extensive vocabulary — is harder to learn than Chinese. So if the Chinese can learn English — as ten-plus million of them have — I should be able to learn Chinese.

While their language might be better than English, when it comes to toilets, the West wins. Inside a toilet block at a market are half a dozen waist-high, door-less cubicles. A single trench beneath them, over which people squat and drop. You would think the dumpers would want the ordeal to be over ASAP, but no one is in a rush; they're chatting and smoking, reading newspapers. They should pay more attention to the task at hand: as much brown matter ends up on the floor as in the trench. No toilet paper, no hosepipe, no bowl. I dread to think how they're wiping clean. I'm not hanging about to find out.

In Kunming's central square, surly police officers patrol with metre-long metal poles in hand. For hitting people, I assume, not for impromptu pole-vaulting. Children holding fishing rods stand around a fountain filled with thousands of goldfish, trying to catch either dinner or a pet. Blind women in white coats give head and shoulder massages — but not toe ones — to people seated on plastic chairs. A guy with no arms sits on the floor with a paint-brush held between his toes and draws intricate Chinese characters on the pavement. If he can write in Chinese despite having no arms, I should soon be able to write a Chinese bestseller.

Near the central square is Green Lake, so-called because the water is green and topped with lily pads, and leafy trees line its walkways and islands. At a corner of the lake, I see a shaven-headed Shaolin monk. A crowd has gathered to watch him. He somersaults and punches, then crouches to pummel bricks with the palms of his hands. He then swigs from a bottle and roars. He next takes three metal rods and bends them around his neck. After a couple of minutes, they're so tightly wrapped that he's gasping for air. Then he sits and meditates.

At a travel agency, I tell them I'd like a train ticket to Chengdu.

"It take twenty hour for go Chengdu. You can hard seater, hard sleeper, or soft sleeper."

"What's the difference between the three?"

"Hard seater, just seat. Many people hard seater. No much space. Hard sleeper, you get bed. Same like bunk bed. One train section have one hundred bed. Soft sleeper, you get bed more nice. Four bed in private section."

"Soft sleeper, please. I don't care what it costs."

The cost is £38. I would have paid three times as much to spend twenty hours with only three Chinese people spitting and smoking and shouting instead of ninety-nine of the buggers doing it.

My bag is scanned and I'm patted down at the entrance to Kunming station. Thousands of people inside. The only white face is mine; it's the world's easiest *Where's Wally?* Police patrol with poles, soldiers stand with guns. It's as safe as it can be, but I take an extra measure: standing in a corner with my arms aloft and one knee raised — à la *Karate Kid* — until it's time to board. The cabin has four beds (two below, two on top); on each is a duvet and pillow. I have it to myself for now, but one local who passes through the carriage notices me and stops to chat. He tells me: "I read Englishman like talk about weather. And social status up, middle, and down is very important ... My favourite English figure is Mr Bean ... Susan Boyle sing nice, but I don't like her face."

The journey is through sprawling agricultural expanses. Not super-sized fields for super-sized farming, but thousands of tiered plots, each no more than ten square metres. Bent-over workers, planting and ploughing, take the place of machinery, making the land look like the world's largest allotment. Mines and factories blemish the beauty; black fumes pump into the grey air. The price to be paid for being the world's workshop.

In the afternoon, three Chinese blokes (twenty to thirty years old) join me in the cabin. The two on the top bunks —

who appear to be mates — peer down at me and gawk like I'm an alien. They've likely never been in close quarters with a foreigner before. One of them — let's call him Chinaman One — gets out his phone and indicates that he wants to take a photo of me. I nod to say it's ok and flash a cheesy smile. He snaps the photo, says "*Khank o*" — an attempt at thank you — and looks pleased with himself, having captured a once-in-a-lifetime picture of a white man in the wild. Later, Chinaman One waves a 100 yuan note at me. I work out that he wants to know if I have any foreign currency. He wants to do an exchange, but I give him a one-dollar note and some Thai coins for free. Minutes later, Chinaman One and his pal — Chinaman Two — have left their beds and are down on mine, sat either side of me. I use Google Maps on Chinaman One's phone to show them where I'm from, and they pore over my passport, carefully turning the pages like it's the world's oldest book. Chinaman Two admires my beard, while Chinaman One takes great pride in showing me his tattoos. At one point, Chinaman Two goes to the restaurant carriage to buy beers, beef jerky, and chicken knees for us to share. After eating, the three of us pose for photos with each other. Then Chinaman One types out "I love you" on his phone and hands it to me. He's fast-tracking the relationship. He might propose before we arrive in Chengdu. More photos while I smoke with them at the end of the carriage. A ticket inspector walks past and wants in on the action. Between them, they manage to ask, "China good? China Bad?"

"China good," I say. And I'm not saying it to be polite. So far, China has been good — and not one of the locals has tried to kill me.

I've had a great time with these guys. The differences between us are more superficial than they are substantial. If you take the time to try to get to know people, I think that's true for everyone, everywhere.

CHENGDU

I'm staying at a £6-a-night hostel nestled within a district of dated flats, accessed by passing through side streets too thin to fit a car. Around the neighbourhood, people sit outside shops and on street corners, smoking, drinking tea, playing *Mahjong* (a traditional Chinese game played with tiles). They smoke, gamble, move tiles, smoke, sip tea, spit, smoke, and move more tiles. Others, on bicycles and mopeds, work their way around the market stalls that line the streets, stopping to pick up produce to place in their front basket.

I assess the options for breakfast. I decide against intestine soup or the tail of something — or a frog, one of which leaps from a bowl and attempts a getaway but is spotted by the seller and scooped from the mucky floor and chucked back into the bowl. I opt for fried sticky rice, a doughnut-type thing, and a hot bun with a meaty filling. While tasty and cheap, Chinese street food isn't the healthiest and is probably one of the reasons — along with smoking like chimneys — that the average life expectancy in China is five years lower than in many Western countries.

In Tianfu Square in the city centre is a white statue of Mao Tse-Tung: the founding father of modern China who died in 1976. Those who love him say he revolutionised the country and put it on the path to power. Those who hate him say his policies killed millions — sometimes accidentally, sometimes on purpose — and that he destroyed much of China's cultural heritage. While I'm stood deciding whether or not to throw eggs at the Mao statue, a bloke approaches and says, "Today, birthday my girlfriend. You sing happy birthday?"

"Err, ok. Where is she?"

"She not here."

He points to his camera.

"On video?" I ask.

"Yes."

"What's her name?"

He says something longer than two syllables that I forget before he's even finished saying it. Then he says, "Four, two, one."

"Happy birthday to you, happy birthday to you, happy birthday dear Chinawoman, happy birthday to you."

Near Tianfu Square is Chunxi, a shopping district with

long, wide streets of clothes stores: H&M, Zara, Rolex, Armani, and Calvin Klein are just some of them. I thought there would be something in the Communist Manifesto that banned the sale of undies for £20 a pair. Hordes of people are shopping, splurging. So you can stop shedding tears — as I know you do — for Chinese people slaving in sweat-shops, doing 18-hour shifts, seven days a week. They're not crying and moaning, looking longingly through brochures of America and Europe. From what I've seen, Chengdu is better than Birmingham and Manchester. Fewer boarded-up shops, homeless people, and beat-up cars; more designer stores and impressive buildings; and public transport is in better condition and cheaper. Countries in the West need to pull their heads out of the sand. They're getting left behind. If it carries on as it is, in fifty years, Westerners might find *they're* crying and moaning, looking longingly through brochures of China.

I take the metro to People's Park, which is packed even though it's 11 am on Monday. Some are strolling; others — mostly old-timers — do activities like dancing and tai chi (even kung fu). Chinese pensioners are an active bunch: I've seen loads pump iron in the exercise yards that are common in Chinese neighbourhoods. I wonder what herbs they're putting in their tea and how legal they are. In the middle of the park is a traditional teahouse with a few dozen people sat on chairs outside. I take a seat and order a tea for £1 — and hope that I've chosen one of those that power grannies to bench press and kick ass. As I sip the tea, a man with a flashlight on his head and an odd metal utensil in his hand shows me a card that says in English that he provides an ear-cleaning service for £2. My ears could do with a clean, having accumulated months of filth — and possibly an insect or two. But is a teahouse the right time and place? No, it's not. What is it with Asians doing what should be private — ear-cleaning, pedicures, pooping — in front of others? I tell him no thanks, but someone nearby takes him up on his offer. He does a thorough job. Perhaps too thorough: the utensil is so far into the woman's right ear that it's verging on poking out the left.

As I continue around the park, I come across hundreds

of lonely hearts ads on laminated A4 paper attached to bamboo poles stuck in the ground and hung from string tied between trees. One has an English translation.

"Local Unmarried Girl

Was born on September 28, 1985. 1.66 metres tall. Bachelor's degree. She is a veteran working in the state's financial department (Chengdu) in Sichuan. She has good looks, elegant temperament, good family upbringing.

Will Be Marry With

The one should be born in 1976-1985, with the height over 1.75 m and outstanding ability. And have the sense of responsibility and good family upbringing. Good health, no bad habits, and who is willing to live with family."

A woman taps my arm and points at the ad; she pulls a photo album from her bag and motions that I should look at it. She's much older than the 1985 date of birth in the ad, so I assume it's for her daughter. I browse the album that contains about twenty photos; on every other page, I give a thumbs-up or say "beautiful". In truth, though, we're talking 4/10 — at best. She didn't mention that in the ad. Still, maybe I'll give her a go. I'm thirty-one and unmarried. The clock is ticking. I recheck her list of requirements to see if I make the grade:

Born between 1976-1985?
Yes.
Taller than 1.75 metres?
Yes.
Outstanding ability?
Yes.
Sense of responsibility?
No. I point at that line on the ad and make a pained expression to indicate that I'm not up to scratch.

Later I visit the Chengdu Research Base of Giant Panda Breeding — home to the largest number of captive giant pandas in the world. It's like a zoo that only has pandas in it. There are no bars or cages, though; the pandas have large, leafy enclosures built into what would be their natural habitat. Giant pandas need places like this because they're an endangered species. Few of them are left: two thousand in the wild and three hundred in captivity. This site began in

1987 with six giant pandas; it now has more than eighty — a result of rescues and romances. They reintroduce pandas into the wild where possible and also rent them to other zoos to raise funds. Panda pimping is ethically dubious, but at least they're doing it for a good cause. They have a few baby pandas: super cute with their fluffy fur and black eyes. For £190, you can hold one and have your photo taken with it. For that price, I'd expect not only to hold it and snap a photo but to have it barbecued and served on a plate. At one point, I pass a line of a hundred-plus school kids that are looked after not by teachers but by soldiers. A couple of the children shriek "hello" at me as I walk by, to which I respond likewise — though with less volume. My reply sets them off like falling dominoes, one by one squealing at me until I've passed them all. Signs say to keep quiet, but keeping a hundred-plus six-year-olds quiet when to their left is a foreigner and to their right are pandas pooping is a task beyond all two million of the Chinese army.

Back at the hostel, I chat to the owner — Susu — who speaks perfect English. I need to book my next train ticket, so it's crunch time on whether to head north-west through Xinjiang to Kazakhstan or to go north-east to Mongolia.

Susu says, "Even though it's dangerous, you can go to Xinjiang. The separatists risk losing international support if foreigners get hurt."

It's not a ringing endorsement, but I'll roll with it. A decision that hopefully won't roll me into an early grave.

Susu takes me to a travel agency to buy a ticket for the train to Urumqi, the capital of Xinjiang. The travel agent says — via Susu — that flying from Chengdu to Urumqi costs only £20 more than taking the train and that flying takes four hours, whereas the train takes forty-eight. Susu tells me I'm a fool for taking the train, and I think I'm a fool for taking the train, but I buy the £80 train ticket anyway.

As I use the internet in the evening, I sometimes forget that Facebook is blocked, and I try to load the site. There's no message to say it's blocked; it just won't load. The Chinese aren't having their human rights abused, though, by being denied photos of cute cats. They have the world's largest online community: hundreds of millions. They use

Chinese alternatives to Facebook and Twitter, like Qzone and Sina Weibo. The government permit usage of those social networks because — unlike the Western ones — they can get full access to the data as and when they want, without explanation. The Chinese government also has thousands of cyber police whose job it is to monitor websites and social networks. They use a filtering system to sort through the billions of posts made each day; it searches for combinations of keywords deemed socially or politically sensitive. For example: Tiananmen Square. Unarmed students. Chinese soldiers. If someone posts criticism of the government, it'll be quickly deleted. Do it repeatedly, and they'll get a midnight knock on their door and not be seen again for a while.

The cyber police haven't censored articles about the latest terrorist incident, which happened yesterday. The attack in Guangzhou again took place at a train station. It's being pinned on the Muslim separatist movement in Xinjiang. I wonder, though, with all the attacks taking place at train stations if bus drivers are to blame, annoyed at people taking trains instead of buses. The terrorists only stabbed people — instead of stabbing *and* bombing. But the kicker for me is that a Westerner was one of those attacked, which didn't happen with previous incidents. That's now three terrorist attacks at railway stations in the last seven weeks, with thirty-five killed and more than two hundred injured. And tomorrow I'm taking a train to the capital of the province responsible for the attacks.

URUMQI

I'm near the end of my 48-hour journey from Chengdu to Urumqi, on which I've crossed countryside, lunar-like expanses, snow-covered mountain ranges. Unlike the Australian outback, where there were massive distances between signs of life, here, there's always some settlement or structure in sight. I haven't had a shower (there are none on board), and I haven't changed my clothes (no one else has), but I've slept well and feel good. I would happily spend forty-eight hours more on here because being on here means I'm not yet where I'm headed — and fuck knows what awaits me there. I've no right to be in this part of China. There's a definite chance that the police or army — who will be in numbers at Urumqi railway station — won't take kindly to me being there. Being locked up and then deported isn't a remote possibility.

The train arrives at Urumqi a couple of minutes ahead of schedule — impressive for a 48-hour trip. A half-hour train ride in the UK normally arrives late. Dozens of police line the platform, directing people to one exit. They yell at anyone dawdling. I attract stares from them, but none approach. Outside, rows of bulletproof-vest-wearing soldiers with automatic weapons and riot shields form a cordon around the entrance. On the other side of the cordon stands a crowd of scruffy, irate men with moustaches and ill-fitting suits. They shout and wave fists in the air. I beeline for the exit gap in the cordon, and the bus stop a couple of metres behind. A bus is about to depart; I've no idea where it's going, but I board it — anywhere is better than here.

I get off the bus somewhere central-looking and wander around trying to orientate myself — difficult when the street signs are in Chinese. After a long walk and a taxi ride and then a second long walk, I find the hotel I pre-booked: Yijia Chain Hotel Lijing Boutique Hotel. It's the first hotel I've come across that has the word *hotel* twice in its name. The Chinese haven't gotten to grips with naming things. Somewhere in China will be a place called Hotel Hotel Hotel.

Half the people in Urumqi don't look Chinese at all. They look more like Borat-does-Islam than the guy you buy chow mien from. They stare at me, as do the soldiers stood on street corners beside tanks — turrets manned and primed to shoot. I should stay indoors as much as I can. It's risky being here at all, and there's no point taking further risks by swanning around for the sake of it. But I'll need to be out and about a bit to get a visa for Kazakhstan. Like China, they're stingy with their visas and don't hand them out willy-nilly to the likes of me.

After two hours of searching for the Kazakhstan consulate, I turn a corner and see a crowd of at least a hundred trying to force their way into a couple of dreary buildings in a manner that makes Black Friday shoppers look like pensioners at the post office. This must be the place. When a guard emerges from one of the doors, people surge at him: they shake their paperwork and shout their plea. A few are let in; the rest are left to wait. A noticeboard is between the buildings, but none of the notices are in English, so I'm unsure which door I need to "queue" at. I make a guess and join the scrum.

After thirty minutes of elbow jabbing and shoulder barging — during which I make little progress — I see that two white faces have appeared in the crowd at the other door. I walk over to them, hoping they can shed some light on the situation. Tash says this is the building for foreigners to apply for a visa. Her friend Callum is a giant of a man and is towards the front of the mob, making full use of his height and weight advantage. Tash shouts encouragement: "Come on, Callum. Push them out the way. You're bigger than them."

Twenty minutes later, a guard comes out and says — according to Callum's translation — to leave and come back tomorrow.

At the hotel, I feel ill and start to sneeze. I go to a pharmacy, but language confusion means that I leave with nothing. I make do with a can of Red Bull from a street stall. Rather than making me feel better, it only makes me sneeze faster. I spend the evening speed-sneezing, watching Fashion TV (the only English-speaking channel out of about seven hundred), and researching why Xinjiang is a battleground reaching boiling point. To summarise: Xinjiang is home to an ethnic group called Uyghurs, whose language, customs, and religion are closely aligned with Turkic countries like Kazakhstan, Afghanistan, Kyrgyzstan, Tajikistan, and Pakistan. From time to time, the Uyghurs had their own homeland, independent from China; most recently from 1944-1949, when Xinjiang was a country called Second East Turkestan Republic. China seized back the land in 1949. They took Tibet a year later. Both Xinjiang and Tibet want to be independent, but China won't give up the two mineral-rich provinces. The Uyghurs and Tibetans can't force out the Chinese, but neither will they submit to them. The result is a strained stalemate. To gain independence, the Tibetans prefer diplomacy, whereas the Uyghurs favour a more radical approach: bombing and stabbing. Both methods have their merits but have proved equally ineffective: neither country is closer to independence now than they were sixty years ago.

Neither has any chance of a referendum on independence, like Scotland will have later this year. Every time Braveheart aired on BBC Two, they piped up about it, and we've at last said we'll let them vote on it if they agree that we'll never again have to watch Mel Gibson wear a skirt. Polls predict that the majority of the tartan-wearing Nessie-shaggers will vote YES! for it. But how long will it last? Once they've spunked all of their North Sea oil money on whisky and Andy Murray merchandise, they'll ask to rejoin the UK. And we'll have to let them: not to do so is akin to not letting your retarded brother back in the house after he ran away with a £5 note in one hand and his willy in the other.

I also learn that Urumqi is 2,500-plus kilometres from the nearest coastline, making it further from the sea than any other city in the world. So while terrorist attacks might be a problem, tsunamis won't be.

I'm back at the Kazakhstan consulate, tackling a rabble as large and riotous as yesterday. But with Callum psyched-up like a man possessed, we get inside within an hour. It transpires, however, that in this building, we can only fill in the visa form and get it reviewed. The application must be submitted in the other building. The other door doesn't have a guard outside it but is enclosed in a cage. The cage isn't locked, but the cage door can only be opened from the inside. Some people enter the cage as others exit from it, and go inside the building. Four times out of five, they get kicked out seconds later, but sometimes they stay inside, encouraging others to try their luck. After an hour, we join one such raid on the door with three Uzbekistanis. We make it inside, but a guard chucks us out. A minute later, the door opens, and the guard lets the three Uzbekistanis in but blocks us. "Fuck you. You're a cunt," shouts Callum in his impenetrable Glaswegian accent. If the guard had understood what he said, that outburst would have earned us an extra week of waiting.

Over the next ninety minutes, we make three more raids on the door; we get kicked out again each time. We're at last let in and submit our application, but it's not yet job done: the clerk tells me, "Come back 22nd. You get visa then."

"That's nine days away. I can't wait that long."

"Come back 22nd. You get visa then."

"Can I pay more to get it in a few days?"

"Come back 22nd. You get visa then."

This means nine more days in Urumqi trying not to get killed. And I have only eleven days left on my Chinese visa. If I come back in nine days and they tell me I can't have a visa or I need to wait longer for it, I'll have no choice but to fly out of China.

As I walk out, feeling sorry for myself, I scan the scrums and note the anguish on the people's faces, many of whom were here yesterday. As frustrating as my experience here has been, I think, as a foreigner, I got preferential treatment. These poor sods could be coming back for days — or even weeks. And they have a good reason for wanting to go to Kazakhstan: to apply for asylum. Whereas Callum, Tash, and I are just going there on a jolly.

Even though my visa isn't confirmed, I decide to buy a ticket for the bus to Kazakhstan because if I wait until I get the visa, the bus might already be fully booked. A barbed-wire perimeter surrounds the bus station. Two tanks and even more soldiers than there were at the train station. Cars are searched, and people are scanned. Everyone is asked for ID; when a soldier puts his hand out for mine, I reach for my pocket but then remember that my passport is at the Kazakhstan consulate. I have no other ID. "No-e speak-e Chinese-e. Me-e English-e. Me-e no-e ID-e," I say, thinking that adding an *e* to the end of words will somehow make them comprehensible.

He looks at me, expressionless; his hand is still outstretched.

I point to my flip-flops and repeat what I said before, but

this time I adopt a new tactic: "No-a speak-a Chinese-a. Me-a English-a. Me-a no-a ID-a."

He waves me past, probably thinking me a syndrome, not a terrorist.

Problems inside, too: the timetables and ticket counter signage are in Chinese and Uyghur. I'm yet to learn my first Chinese character. I've been too busy watching Fashion TV. I join one of the queues; I get to the front and hand over a piece of paper stating my destination — Almaty — and departure date. The ticket clerk looks at it, then stares blankly at me. I say "Almaty" in as many ways and tones as I can think of. One of them, she finally understands.

"No, you ...," she says and points at the exit, twisting her hand to the right.

Outside, I wander around saying, "Bus. Almaty. Ticket," to anyone who'll listen — which isn't many. It's not a good spot to be dilly-dallying. Soldiers keep a keen eye on me, including one that's manning the turret of a tank. He's not likely to shoot me, but he might do if he's bored or thinks that he'll get a medal. Through hand gestures and piecing together the odd word of broken English, I work out that this isn't even the right bus station. This one is for domestic buses; the station for international buses is down the road.

At the right station, I buy a £45 ticket for the 24-hour sleeper bus to Kazakhstan. I'm supposed to collect my visa in nine days at 3 pm, and the bus departs that same day at 6 pm. I'm cutting it close but want to get moving ASAP. There's only one bus per day. If I wait until the day after, with then only a day left on my Chinese visa, a breakdown or cancellation will force me to fly.

I check out of my hotel at midday and get to the Kazakhstan consulate — backpack with me — at 1 pm. I'm cold and wet when I arrive and have to wait in the rain — no cover provided. Tash and Callum aren't here today because they don't need their visa as urgently as I do. But I'm not alone in a mob of moustaches. With me are Jared and Kate, a couple from New Zealand who are bicycling around Asia.

"It's terrible what happened this morning, all those people being killed," says Jared, to which I look confused. He says, "At the morning market by Renmin Park, two cars drove along the street throwing explosives out the window. More than thirty people were killed. It's been all over the news."

That park is only a kilometre from the hotel I've been staying at. I was there yesterday.

Jared's got more bad news: "We came here yesterday to collect our visas, which was the date they told us to come when we submitted our documents, but the guards came outside and shooed everyone away."

If that happens today, I'm screwed.

At 4.15 pm — fifteen minutes before the consulate closes for the day, and with not a single person allowed inside since I arrived — a guard opens the door to let in some people. Jared and Kate squeeze in, but not me. When I do make it in, a guard inside kicks a bunch of us back out.

All looks lost.

Then Jared appears at the door; he holds aloft not one passport but two. "Mate, I've got your passport. It's got your visa in it."

He's a gift from the gods, delivered by bicycle. I thank Jared for his help, then push on to the bus station. It's on the other side of the city, and I have to negotiate a rainy rush hour for a bus that departs in an hour and a half.

I get there just in time, soaked and shivering — which on a scale of one to ten for states in which to turn up for a 24-hour bus ride ranks as a two, with the only state worse being soaked, shivering, and bollock-naked.

KAZAKHSTAN

URUMQI TO ALMATY

Three chunky, stubbled Uzbekistanis drive the bus; they rotate between driving and sleeping. Whoever's driving always has a ciggy on the go. The other passengers are a motley crew of Kazakhstanis, Kyrgyzstanis, Uzbekistanis. One looked a stunner at the outset but now looks the opposite. A 24-hour across-Asia journey should be part of Miss World. (With a bit of make-up, even I can look good on stage in a bikini for an hour.) I lie in my bed, face pressed against the window, peering at a Narnia-like landscape covered in thick snow and fir trees. I look for fairies and fauns but see only sheep and horses. An occasional wigwam-type structure, smoke billowing from its top; outside them stand fur-clad blokes, readying themselves for a day of hunting unicorns.

The scenery since I left Sydney has varied wildly. As snapshots, the landscapes contrast as much as black and white, but they blend and merge so slowly and subtly that the transition from desert to jungle to Narnia unfolds unnoticed. To fly from place to place might be quicker, but it means missing everything in between, and there can be as much to enjoy between destinations as there is in them; like today's scenery, which is as spectacular as I've ever seen. A just reward for seeing through those tough days in Urumqi, which made me doubt if this trip was worth the hassle. Seeing scenes like these reminds me that it is.

On entering Kazakhstan, we cross flat, bare land for hours; the nothingness alleviated only by cloud-topped mountains in the distance — and the odd camel. A whopper of a country, it has more space than it knows what to do with. It's the size of these countries combined: Italy, Spain, France, Norway, Sweden, Germany, and the UK. At the bus station in Almaty, dozens harass me with offers of taxis and hotels. I make a deal with one to take me to a hostel. When I'm in the taxi, I realise that it's not a taxi, just a man who owns a car. Fearing that he might plan to rob me, I jut out my chin and growl — a tactic I use to sucker people into thinking that I'm a double-hard bastard. I've never been robbed, so the strategy is scientifically proven. I'm taken to Hostel 74/76. If they couldn't choose between calling it Hostel 74 or Hostel 76, they should have split the difference and called it Hostel 75. The room costs £7 a night. I'm sharing it with a couple of Russians and a Kazakh.

The Kazakh — Saken — invites me to go with him to Ile Alatau: a mountain on the fringe of the city. I'm not equipped for mountains, but the sun's shining, and it's thirtyish degrees. A series of cable cars take us up. At 2,000 metres is Shymbulak: Central Asia's premier skiing resort. A sign displays equipment rental costs; you can hire everything you need for £15 a day. In the Alps, an apple costs £15. As we rise higher, Saken tells me about a business deal he's working on: "We want to buy 2,400 cows. Each costs £3,000; that's the price for a Canadian cow, which have the best DNA. At first, we'll sell the milk abroad to be processed; later, we'll build a processing plant here. As well as selling the milk, we'll also breed the cows and sell some of the calves, and slaughter the older cows and sell the meat."

A good idea. When I return to Birmingham, I'll go to the bank and ask for £6,000 to buy two cows. This time next year, I'll be a millionaire.

The final cable car stop — at 3,200 metres — is Talgar Pass. The peak of the mountain, a hundred metres away, pokes into the clouds. It's damn cold; snow covers the ground. But as we're here, we may as well take a walk. After twenty minutes — five spent making a snow angel — my face is red, my lips have cracked, my feet feel like stone. We take refuge on an out-of-service chairlift to get my feet out of the snow. Saken asks why I don't have any trainers.

I tell him: "If I buy trainers, I'll also have to buy socks. And a shoe rack and a sock drawer. It's a slippery slope."

On the bus back to the hostel, a guy wearing a baseball cap and baggy jeans comes over. After he asks where I'm from and what I'm doing in Almaty, he says he wants to go to Los Angeles to be a rapper.

I ask, "You'll rap in English?"

"No. Rap Kazakh language."

"Why Los Angeles?"

"American girl. Ass is big. And ears. I like."

"Big ears?"

"Yes."

"You mean big eyes?"

I point to his eyes and say "eyes", then I point to his ears and say "ears".

He pulls his ears with his hands and says, "No, big ears."

I later go to the train station to buy a ticket to Astana, the capital of Kazakhstan. The ticket-seller doesn't speak English, but she puts me on the phone with a woman who speaks a little, and that woman relays what I want back to the ticket-seller. The ticket is for a day earlier than I wanted, and I don't know if I've got a seat or a bed, and I think I was overcharged, but at least I've got one.

Back at the room, Saken picks up the ticket; he says, "I thought you were travelling without flying."

"Yeah, I am."

"But this is a plane ticket to Astana."

"Yeah, right. Funny." But he's not a joker. And he's not smiling. "What?! Are you sure?"

"The arrival time is an hour after the departure. And see here, it says 'airport' in English."

"Ah, shit, so it does."

I didn't check the ticket after the seller gave it to me because I assumed it was all in Kazakh. I also assumed, it being a railway station, that they wouldn't be selling fucking aeroplane tickets.

ALMATY

The woman at the railway station — who Saken phoned to explain the mix-up — laughs at me when I walk in. She gives me a refund and points to a row of nearby counters. I realise the mistake I made: this is a travel agency within the railway station. Probably dozens of people every day make the exact mistake that I did. Though maybe not; maybe I'm just an idiot. At one of the counters, I hand over a piece of paper on which Saken has written in Kazakh what I want and pay £20 for the train ticket to Astana — twenty hours away. I'll wait until I'm in Astana until I celebrate — in case this is a camel ticket, not a train one.

I next go to a subway station to travel to the immigration office that foreigners have to report to within five days of entering the country. At the ticket barrier, I'm accosted by a brawny guard. I don't understand what he says other than the word "passport". I hand it to him; he turns to the photo page. He looks confused, then gestures me to follow him. We walk down a corridor and into a small room; on the walls are mugshots. He radios someone else to come. When his comrade arrives, he shows him my passport, which he scrutinises. A discussion between the pair, during which both look me up and down and frown. "UK?" the first man asks me.

"Yes," I tell him.

"London?" he asks.

"Yes."

(I'm really from Birmingham, but I've told loads of people I've met on this trip that I'm from London. Tuk-tuk drivers, suit-sellers, waiters, and the like don't know Birmingham; it lacks the football and musical celebrity of its brothers Liverpool and Manchester. So for the sake of simplicity, I say London; to avoid getting caught up in nonsense conversations ...

"Mister, you where from?"

"I'm from England."

"London, yes?"

"No. Birmingham."

"Burning ham? You burn ham why?"

"Not burning ham. Birmingham."

"I no understand."

"Birmingham. I'm from Birmingham."

"Birmingham in London?"

"No, it's a city two hours from London."

"I no understand."

"London is one city. Birmingham is another city. I'm from Birmingham. It's 200 km from London."

"London, yes?"

"Are you fucking with me?"

"Again, please."

"Are you— Look, I'm from Birmingham. B-I-R-M-I-N-G-H-A-M. It's a city in England, and that's where I'm from. Birmingham, not London."

"I no understand."

"Ok, you win: I'm from London.")

The guard screws up his face as he points at my beard and flip-flops. He shakes his head like I'm a lost cause; then, he waves me away.

I blame Beckham; he's inflated the expected sartorial standards of overseas British blokes. Borat has maybe had the reverse effect for Kazakhs, who when abroad are quizzed why they're not wearing a mankini.

In the queue at the immigration office, I chat to a stringy, pony-tailed Frenchman called Cedric. He tells me that he walked here from France: "I set off two years ago. I walk 25 km most days, but it can be up to 40 km if I'm short on supplies. I camp outdoors sometimes; other times, locals invite me to stay with them."

When I ask where he'll finish, he says, "I don't know. I'll just keep heading eastwards."

It sounds unbelievable, but I believe him. If you saw him, you'd also believe him. He looks like someone who's spent two years walking. He smells like it too. But I do some sums to check: Paris to Almaty is about 7,000 km, and he said he set off two years ago; it works out to an average of 10 km a day. Definitely doable.

Talking to him makes me think: What a lightweight I am, taking trains and buses. Not even cycling.

You might question why I'm not cycling — like Jared and Kate are, as well as some other long-distance overlanders I've met at times — and the answer to that is: as a man who can't ride a bike (not even for three metres) it would be very fucking difficult to ride one for 13,000+ kilometres from Australia to Europe. I could have done it on a child's bicycle with stabilisers, but can you imagine the commotion that would cause, me — a thirty-one-year-old white man — riding through the boonies of China on a little pink bike? All 1.3 billion people in China would have stopped working to come to look at me. If the elements and distance didn't kill me, the embarrassment would have.

My Mum tells people that I never learnt when I was a child because I liked to keep my socks clean; that when she tried to teach me how to ride a bike, I got oil on my socks and cried and refused to get back on. I don't remember that at all. I only recall being seven or eight and not being able to ride one and already thinking I was then too old for stabilisers. I've always denied the dirty socks story — and claim the real reason I was never taught to ride a bike is that as the middle child I was neglected and that it's a miracle I can even walk — but maybe she is telling the truth: that would explain my dedication to flip-flops — so I can avoid the irksome issue of keeping my socks clean. But why would I care about dirty socks when I don't care about my jeans being dirty? To find the truth of the matter, I'll have to buy some socks and get them dirty. If I don't break down in tears, I'll sue my Mum for slander.

In the afternoon, I go to a spa complex called Arasan Baths. It has separate sections for women and men; in the men's section, everyone is say-hello-to-Mr-Wonka, birthday-suit starkers. I take a seat in a sauna, in which are three other guys. After a minute, two of them stand: one bends over, and the other beats the bent man's back and arse with a bundle of birch twigs. After that pair of pervs have gone, I'm left with one guy: a Carlo Ancelotti lookalike. He points at the coals and asks me something. I tell him that I'm from England, that I can't speak Kazakh.

He barks at me: "You think your country important? Everybody have to speak English? Your English no good here. You speak Kazakh."

We eyeball each other in silence. I think to myself: If he tries to push my face into the coals, I'll blind him with birch twigs.

Then, his tone changes — like a switch has been flicked — and I'm his new best friend. He tells me he was an officer in the Soviet Union for twenty-five years and worked in Afghanistan, Tajikistan, Germany, and Hungary. He invites me to drink tea with him. We walk out of the sauna and into a cafe, each grabbing a towel on the way to wrap around our waists. He orders two beers, no tea. He downs half his beer in one go. I do the same.

"Communist life like prison life," he says. "No freedom and food not enough. But vodka, have a lot. We think it last forever, then one day, 1991, it no more. They say money finished, Soviet Union finished. I come back Kazakhstan and become businessman."

He necks the rest of his beer and orders two more.

"British people are best," he tells me. "Men are like stone. Nation of fighter, of adventurer. Look at you, here alone in Kazakhstan. Don't know language, don't know anyone, but don't care. You good example of British."

He again downs half his beer. So do I.

He says, "World has to beware Russia; they are like angry bear. World worry China, but Russia is most dangerous. I like America more. They welcome everybody. Live together in peace."

Fifteen minutes after we sit, and having drunk two beers each, we leave the cafe and spend an hour rotating through steam rooms, saunas, pools. After two more hasty beers and getting changed back into clothes, he says I must join him to eat. As we dine and drink — four more beers — he talks about his shrapnel wounds, his son's wheeling and dealing in oil, and Jamie Oliver (who he thinks is the best chef in the world). He insists on paying the bill and also that I go to his home to meet his wife.

We drive to a bleak estate of high-rises. While trying to park, he scrapes another vehicle; he says, with a flick of the hand, "That was already bloody shit car." Inside, I meet his wife and daughter, a pair of plump women wearing paisley dresses. We sit at the kitchen table for a few hours, eating, drinking, chatting. I tell him I'll get a taxi back to the hostel, but he won't hear of it; he insists on driving me himself.

He turned out to be alright. I'm glad I didn't blind him with birch twigs.

ASTANA

My hostel is on the twelfth floor of a block of flats. I'm sharing a four-bed room with three twenty-something Kazakh blokes, who rolled in at 5 am. Two are snoring, and the other is sleeping naked (without a sheet to cover him). Among the other guests are a couple of Russian identical twins. At first, I didn't know they were twins, as I hadn't seen both of them in the same room at the same time. I thought it was one person who kept changing his clothes. There's also a Ghanaian who's in Astana to set up a program to cross-promote Kazakhstan and Ghana. He tells me: "If we educate people about the other country, it will create interest to travel there. I'll hire some rooms and show movies; this will help them learn." I'm not convinced that showing *The Lion King* in Kazakhstan and *Borat* in Ghana will help much. That said, I've watched *Borat*, and now I'm in Kazakhstan; while I've never watched *The Lion King* and haven't visited Africa. So there might be something in it.

The Ishim River bisects Astana, and the two sides could hardly be more different. One side is an unremarkable, Soviet-style affair; the other is sci-fi-like, shades of Las Vegas and Dubai. The Palace of Peace and Reconciliation is an epic shiny pyramid. The Bayterek Tower is a tall white tower topped by a golden globe. The Khan Shatyr is a tent-type structure that looks like something the Teletubbies would live in. There's also a presidential palace that looks like the White House, a flying-saucer-shaped circus, a couple of egg-shaped buildings, and more skyscrapers than I can count. Adding to the wacky factor is Astana's location: in the middle of the world's largest steppe. For a thousand kilometres in every direction is a desolate expanse. The city has a clear-cut boundary where buildings and roads stop; then, nothing but nothingness.

The bling of the capital is a consequence of Kazakhstan becoming a top-table baller in oil and gas. In 2000, the world's largest oil find of the last thirty years was made in the country. Since then, warp speed change. Before that, Astana hardly existed. Then called Akmola, it was inhabited primarily by impoverished agricultural workers and was known only for once being a gulag. President Nazarbayev instigated the change. Deciding that the former capital — Almaty — was too close to China, he granted capital status to Akmola and forced tens of thousands of government employees to move here. A year later, it was renamed Astana, which sounds like a cool name but in Kazakh means "capital city".

At the Russian embassy, I'm told that to get a visa for Russia I must show proof of residence in Kazakhstan for the last three months. I'm well short of that with nineteen days left on my Kazakh visa, so to travel to Europe via Russia — the most direct route — is ruled out. Kazakhstan to Azerbaijan is the next best option. That route hinges on getting a visa for Azerbaijan; to get one of those, I need a letter of invitation from someone in Azerbaijan. Google tells me that I can buy a letter of invitation for £35. The websites selling them all seem likely to steal my identity after I send them copies of my documents, but I've no choice but to risk it. If they steal my identity, I'll just steal someone else's. (I quite fancy being a Fijian woman.)

I received a PDF copy of my letter of invitation to Azerbaijan and spent yesterday locating the Azerbaijan embassy; once there, I was told the lazy sods are only open on Mondays, Wednesdays, and Fridays and only from 3-5 pm on those days.

I'm back there again today. Not a dreary building swarmed by hundreds, but a pink house with a handful of people politely queuing. In the waiting room, an old man says to me: "Liverpool. Champion?"

"No," I tell him. "Manchester City."

Silence for a minute. Then he asks, "Margaret Thatcher?"

When I swipe my finger across my neck to show that she's dead, he looks even sadder. His radio must have broken in 1990, and he's yet to buy a new one.

No faffing with counter clerks; I'm called through to meet the head honcho: the Azerbaijan Ambassador. He's dressed like a waiter in a third-rate restaurant. Paper is stacked and strewn across the floor. He checks my paperwork while fielding phone calls and signing documents brought into him. He tells me, "Come back after Wednesday."

"After Wednesday? So Friday?"

"Between Wednesday and Friday."

"Thursday? But you're not open on Thursday."

"Between Wednesday and Thursday."

A week has passed since I submitted my visa application. If I don't get the visa today, my hopes of leaving Kazakhstan without flying crash from small to zero. It's not possible to extend a Kazakh tourist visa, and there are only seven days left on mine. In that time, I need to travel the breadth of the country to the port city of Aktau and board a vessel bound for Azerbaijan (which doesn't have a land border with Kazakhstan). That boat could be a problem. The best news I can find online is that a boat from Aktau to Azerbaijan leaves every three to fourteen days; the worst is that boats allowing passengers onboard no longer travel that route. Less than three weeks after I danced with defeat in Urumqi, I'm back on the ropes, about to be KO'd.

At the embassy, I'm called through to see the ambassador. "Is the visa ready?" I ask after he's finished a series of calls.

He says nothing but delves into one of the many mounds of documents spread across the floor. He finds my passport and flicks through it. "Your visa, hmm, I don't know," he says, looking puzzled. He digs into another mound and pulls out a slip of paper with my photo on it. He picks up a glue stick and makes the two into one.

Game on.

Saken — the guy I made snow angels with in Almaty — lives in Astana, so I ask him to come with me to buy a ticket for the train to Aktau. (With only a week left on my visa, I can't afford any plane ticket errors.) The options are a £110 first-class ticket to Atyrau in north-west Kazakhstan tomorrow, then a train south from there to Aktau; or wait three days for a cheaper ticket for a direct train to Aktau. It's more hassle and more expensive, but those two days saved by going via Atyrau could be crucial. I'd be gutted to reach Aktau and find I've missed the boat by a day or two and that it was scrimping and laziness that felled me. So I book the ticket to Atyrau.

ATYRAU TO AKTAU

I arrived in Atyrau yesterday afternoon after a 22-hour trip. My first-class cabin — in which I was alone — was great: it had an ensuite. I felt better when I got off the train than when I got on, which is a first.

Back with the common people for today's train: an ex-Soviet special with dark woods, brown carpets, ruby-red upholstery. I'm in *kupe* class, which means a cabin with four beds. I while away the hours with walks of the train — prying into cabins through wide-open doors, glimpsing people eating, chatting, sleeping — and by staring out the window at mainly nothing. The emptiness is interrupted only by the occasional one-horse town, all of which we stop at. At one of these, the town's one horse is temporarily joined by another two hundred, herded past by men riding bareback, brandishing heavy sticks. Any horse that hints at fleeing to freedom is thwacked. They should chance it because they're destined for a dinner plate: horse is the meat of choice for Kazakhs. For a while, I stroke my beard — which is larger than it ever has been, and which I'll have to shave before I return to the UK, so MI5 don't think I've turned to the dark side, have been away on a tour of jihadi training campuses — and decide with hours to burn I'll finally answer the question we all have: the meaning of life. After careful thought, I decide it's, To be yourself, you can't be no one else. (It's quite similar to the opening line of *Supersonic* by Oasis — the song I was listening to prior to pondering the meaning of life — but that's probably just a coincidence.)

On one walk of the train, I meet a fella called Azamat, who invites me to his cabin to eat dumplings and drink tea. He tells me: "In August, I'm getting married. I need to work a lot now to pay for it. Kazakh weddings are expensive because you have to invite everyone you know, even if you don't know them well. We have five hundred people on our guest list at the moment, but we expect it to be many more." He's going to a town an hour from Aktau to visit his sister, whose husband died last week in an explosion at the oil refinery he worked at. The company refuses to pay compensation because investigators claim that it was the employees' fault for being drunk at work. "He was Muslim and never once drank alcohol," says Azamat. "The company must have bribed the investigators. It's an injustice; I won't accept it. My sister has four children. I must help them." First, he'll go to local officials to ask for assistance; if they don't help him, he'll go to the media. A high-risk tactic, one that could see him thrown into a van, never to be seen again.

Later, while smoking in the end carriage of the train, a bloke in an Adidas tracksuit speaks to me. When I tell him that I'm from England, he taps his chest and says, "Me Azerbaijan. Name Roma." His gold teeth flash a smile. As he shakes my hand, I notice a stitched-up wound on his. He makes a stabbing gesture to explain the injury, which I guess means someone stabbed him. I tell him that I'm going to Baku in Azerbaijan and that I'm trying to travel by boat. He doesn't understand, so on some paper, I draw a boat.

"Me boat. Me, you, boat," he says and moves his index fingers together to indicate that we can pair up.

"Ok, sure," I tell him. He may have taken the boat before and so will improve my chances.

Back in my cabin, though, paranoia kicks in: What's he involved in that would get him stabbed? Why is he taking the boat when it's faster to fly? Is he smuggling something across the border?

"Come. Taxi in," says Roma, outside Aktau railway station.

I'll give him a chance. What's the worst that could happen? (Actually, let's not think about that.)

Half an hour later, the taxi stops by a small office. I recognise it from a photo in an old blog post I read while researching where to buy the boat ticket. No dice, though; it's boarded-up. We try a few travel agents; none are selling tickets for boats. Then we drive twenty minutes to the port; at the office there, Roma speaks to a woman. "Boat, no. No boat. Boat no go. No go on boat," is Roma's summary afterwards.

Outside by the taxi, Roma says to me, "Give £50."

"£50? What for?"

He points at the taxi and then makes a roof sign with his hands (which I guess to mean hotel). £50 seems a lot, but we've been in the taxi a long time, and I've no idea how much hotels cost here, so I hand over the cash. Forty-five minutes later, on the outskirts of the city, we stop outside a hostel that's part-way through renovation or demolition. Roma pays the driver £15; then we go inside, where a woman takes us to a room with six beds in it. We're the only guests. Roma hands her £10 for the two of us.

Roma says to me, "You go shop. Buy beer."

"Why don't you go to the shop and buy beer?"

"No, you," he snaps back, then adds "please" and a gilded smile.

When I get back from the shop, and we're drinking a couple of beers in the room, he says, "Shirt I need. You give." He grabs one that I've unpacked without waiting for a reply. I don't want to argue with him, so I let it slide.

After the beer, I go to the restaurant that's beside the hostel. I order and sit at a table outside. Soon after, Roma shows up and sits at my table. After he's eaten, he taps his pocket and says, "Money, no. Need more."

"Where's that £50?"

"Gone. Pay taxi. Pay hotel. Give more."

"No."

"Fuck you. Give more."

His mask has more than slipped; it's vanished. What's left isn't pretty. I'm not sure I can take him in a fight, so I tell him that I'll go to the room to get some and will be back soon.

In the room, I consider the situation: there's a bloke out there wearing one of my shirts, with a wedge of my money in his pocket, who wants me to pay for his horse burger. If it carries on like this, in a day or two — if I'm not dead in a ditch — I'll be down to only my boxers and passport. I need to man up, grow some balls. Or pack my bag and run. I do the latter: out the back door and down a dusty road.

A half-hour walk brings me to the main drag. While looking for an internet cafe, I see an Irish pub called The Shamrock that has wifi. I opt for that instead. Over a few pints, my waning morale crashes. I plumb the depths of Google but can't find any up-to-date information about the boat to Baku. After five pints, I've written it off and set about drowning my sorrows.

As I order my eighth pint at the bar, I get talking to Raymond — a fifty-something Scottish fella — who turns out to be the pub's owner. When he tells me that he's lived in Aktau for eight years, I ask him if he knows anything about boats going to Azerbaijan.

He says, "There used to be a boat running between here and Baku, but I haven't heard anyone mention it in a long time. I'll make a few calls to see what I can find out."

The calls yield no leads.

After my tenth lager, my sorrows are drowned. Raymond says I should stay at the Green Hotel; he gets one of his staff to drive me there. At £35 a night, it's not cheap, but sod it: to budget no longer matters. My visa expires in three days. Then I'll fly home.

AKTAU

At 10 am, the ringing of the in-room phone wakes me. I don't understand what the woman on the phone says, so I go down to reception, from where she takes me to the dining room. I'm too sick to stomach breakfast, but it's easier to go with the flow. A minute after I sit down, a broad-chested, stubbly bloke sits at my table and grins at me. He speaks Kazakh into his phone, then hands it to me; on the screen, it says: "I manager hotel. Name Zaurbek. Is your name? Business person? City Aktau good?"

When I start to answer, he indicates that I should speak into the phone so it can translate. With my crippling hangover, I'm not in the mood for this, but I'll have to do it: I can't tell the manager to bugger off. The Google Translate conversation goes on for twenty minutes. When I explain the journey I've been on, he says, "Think you fellows mental. Kazakhstan, no one travel much."

I'm about to excuse myself — so I can return to hiding under my duvet — when he says, "Mike, you need help ticket Azerbaijan?"

I tell him that I've tried, that there's no boat — at least not one that leaves within the next few days.

He says, "Come reception thirty minutes past one hour."

I ride with him in a black Mercedes. He wears shades and smokes — and still beams a smile. He looks like a mafioso on ecstasy. We stop outside the closed office that I came to with Roma. Zaurbek knocks the door and peers through the boarded-up window. After he checks with a nearby office, he says, "No ticket here. Office closed before."

Fifteen minutes later, we're driving in circles. I must appear defeated because Zaurbek says, "Mike, worry not. You go Azerbaijan."

He's called me Mike all morning. I left it too late to correct him.

We find the place he was looking for and go inside and take a seat at a desk. He talks with the woman working there. She starts to fill in a form.

Zaurbek tells me: "Give must passport. Ticket £65."

"It's a boat ticket?" I ask.

"Yes, boat. Maybe today. Maybe tomorrow. Maybe three or four day."

She gives me a ticket; then Zaurbek and I leave.

I'm happy to have a ticket, but I can't quite yet smoke a cigar: there are only two days left on my Kazakh visa, so even though I have a ticket, I won't be able to use it if the boat doesn't depart in the next two days.

In the evening, Zaurbek knocks my door; in his hand is a bottle of whisky. I'm still hungover, but I can't refuse after the help he's given me. Over a few hours, we finish the bottle.

Google Translate has spewed some waffle today — stuff about socks, chalk, lemons — but it hits the spot now: as the boozing concludes, it translates what he says to: "As life happens, we have to help each other."

---

8 pm, the next day: A knock on my door. Zaurbek hands me his phone: "Boat registration. Leaving soon. Come now." He drives me to the port and speaks to someone to double-check my ticket is okay. Without his help, I'd never have made it.

After he leaves, I sit on a plastic chair in the waiting room and watch Colombia play Ivory Coast on a battered television. Six others are here: a family of four Azeris and a couple of Kazakhs. I keep an eye on the door and hope that Roma doesn't show up. That was a gamble when I did a runner. I twisted and got twenty-one. Luck has been on my side: to find The Shamrock; for Raymond to send me to the Green Hotel; for the boat to leave today and not a few days from now.

At 11 pm, I board the Professor Gul: a rusty ferry that flies the Azeri flag. The boat is still docked when I go to bed — in a tiny room shared with the Kazakhs. When I wake, I'll be crossing the Caspian Sea. And in a day, two days maybe, I'll be on the shores of Europe.

As I drift to sleep, I think about the trip: I lost track of how much I spent, but estimate it was £6,000. I'd have spent an equal amount had I stayed in the UK for the time I've been away. It's been money well spent. To spend on enriching experiences makes more sense than spending on anything else, and the experiences on this journey have improved me, made me wiser and stronger. I put myself in the hands of the world and wasn't chewed up and spat out.

Many more wanted to help than to harm. If I'd listened to the scaremongers, I'd never have started; they told me that the world is fraught with danger, that I'd get kidnapped or attacked or robbed, that I'd get injured or sick. But I didn't. To live in fear is to fear life. I've never felt more fearless. I've never felt more alive.

THE END

It starts in El Ceibo and ends in the Amazon; a savage journey in between, by bus and boat through Americas central and south. Along the way, a failed revolution, a spewing volcano, a drawer of cocaine; and a surreal assortment of oddballs and freaks.

www.gonzo.schule/amerzonia

EL CEIBO TO GUATEMALA CITY

A man the size of two men, biceps as thick as my neck. He's at a desk, on a chair large enough to be a throne, staring at me squirm on the sofa. My butt is sticky with sweat from the faux leather. His henchman, who forced me to come to this dingy room, is stood beside him, doubling the sullen eyes on the prey. Door closed. Blinds drawn.

"Pay," he says, his expression emotionless, the perfect poker face.

I say, "I'm not paying."

The more I protest, the less English he speaks, the more bullying his attitude. He soon speaks only Spanish.

I glance at the door: I could make a run for it. But the door may be locked, and I don't know where I can run to. I'm in the middle of nowhere, on the border between Mexico and Guatemala. And on the other side of the door are men with guns.

The room grows smaller with each second, slowly

crushing my defiance. But I have some left: "I'm not paying," I say again.

He scowls, says, "*No pagas, no te vas.*" Don't pay, don't leave. Said with an absoluteness that permits no argument.

Gatekeeper is used as a metaphor; he's a literal one, in charge of this gate out of Mexico. He won't let me leave until I've paid £20 for a tourist permit. But I paid when I entered the country. He knows I've paid: it's impossible to enter Mexico without paying. Under the pretence of officialdom, I'm being mugged. He knows I know there's nothing I can do about it. He's the judge, the jury. If I continue to refuse, he'll tell me to sod off. It took me four hours to get here. To get to another border crossing, I'll have to return to Palenque and travel four-plus hours south from there — where I may have the same issue. Or he'll plant drugs on me. Not a sizeable amount — it wouldn't be believable for me to traffic against the northbound tsunami — but a gram or two he could get away with.

"Can I pay by card?" I ask.

"No."

"Can I get a receipt?"

"No."

I pay. I've no choice.

I call him a twunt as I'm leaving, wrapping it up with a Merry Christmas — "*Feliz Navidad*, you twunt." — to avoid suspicion. It's a safe insult, I think — surely he won't know that? Then I panic that he'll Google it, so I quick-walk off — as fast as I can go without running — past pickup trucks with cargoes of people, past loiterers primed to prey.

I got here — the border at El Ceibo — via a through-the-night journey from Mexico City. Before boarding, airport-style security: IDs checked and bodies frisked, luggage scanned and searched. The driver locked in his cabin, the glass tinted and bulletproof — shielded from bandits and the stink of chow mein, which several passengers brought on board on paper plates from a cafe at one stop. I had a seat next to the bog; if we were ambushed, I could have used it as a panic room. I'd have taken my chances, however, because the toilet was vile, the toxic whiff like a soiled diaper on a warm day. Drop-down screens with volume dialled to granny-friendly prevented sleeping. Now, a battered minivan speeding along a narrow, hole-studded highway to Flores in the north of Guatemala. No one wears a seatbelt because there are none. Trucks hurtle at us, thunder close by; the road barely wide enough to squeeze in a couple of passing vehicles. Some cross their chests, whisper prayers. They're right to do so: beside the road are burnt-out chassis, victims of long-ago crashes. Names of the dead are spelt in stones on the canvases of hillsides.

The station at Flores is a frenetic jigsaw, its many pieces in motion. Dust rises from wheels and footfall; people cover their face, cough and splutter. Some spit, some piss on walls. Shoeshiners struggle for silk purses from pigs' ears; the shinees on wooden thrones, paupers playing princes. A guard outside a shop — one selling day-to-day items not diamonds — shotgun slung about his neck. Pilfer a pack of Oreos: BANG. You're dead. I've no such protection. It's a sad state of affairs when you're worth less than a pack of Oreos. Cries of "*Agua, agua. Fruta, fruta.*" Others stick their head in minivans to peddle socks and batteries, medicines and fireworks. Someone's selling a framed picture of a woman posing sexily on all fours, a waterfall photoshopped in the background.

I board a minivan bound for Sayaxche, south of here on my screenshot of a map of Guatemala. The distance on the map isn't far, but the terrain between there and here is unknown. How long it will take, I've no idea: an hour or seven or twelve. I don't mind. Days like these on the road are some of the best on a trip like this; thinking and observing, channel-surfing, catching glimpses, flashes, bits. I'll ride until darkness draws down a veil, then bed down until sunrise. Where I don't know; I'll deal later with detail. No need to stress: always a town of some sort or size, always a hotel, a store. I won't sleep on the streets. I won't starve.

The van is buggered. One window cracked like a snowflake, stuck with sellotape. Strapped to the roof are suitcases soiled by the decades; also bicycles and sacks of all sorts, tied tenuously in place. My bag is on my lap. Any bigger and it would need to go on top, exposed to thieves, to the elements. It's the litmus test for those who say they travel light: if you're not comfortable with your bag on your lap for hours, it's not light. I have only 7 kg in my bag. I'm without all but the essentials — and also without several essentials: no towel, no trainers, no smartphone. (An iPod Touch is my only tech.) I do at least have footwear beyond flip-flops, having caved in to the demands of civilised society, which deems any man with his toes on show to be a hobo. A wise man packs hiking boots. A wise man I'm not: I've packed Chelsea boots.

Seats soon full. Plastic stools put in the aisle — soon full too. Several stand. One with a chicken; a live one, its feet and beak tied. Quetzales go out through windows; plates of tacos come in. Others buy fried slices of bananas or strawberries coated in chocolate. Crumbs tumble from mouths, adding to those already on the seats and floor. I'd pity the person who had to clean this van if such a person existed. We cruise about town with the door open, scouting for extras. Somehow squeezed in, another four children and three chickens. A butt nudges my face; a baby sucks a breast, close enough for me to suck the other. A girl sings Christmas-sounding songs. I'd prefer a Christmas-sounding silence. All but me are locals. My blue eyes give away that I'm not of this parish, that I'm a wanderer wandering, but no one's bothered about my presence.

I'm taking a locals' *colectivo* — rather than a tourist shuttle — to hide in plain sight. Desperadoes, I reason, are less likely to hijack a minivan of paupers than a busload of foreigners. Still, to be on the safe side, I have money stashed all over: various pockets and parts of my bag — even down my sock. A thief might empty my pockets and take my bag, but steal my socks, surely not. Paranoid? Maybe. But with reason: Guatemala is ranked as one of the twenty-five most dangerous countries in the world. It's fifth for gun-related deaths per 100,000 people. Police are overwhelmed: A force of 30,000 for a population of seventeen million. 90% of homicides remain unsolved. The past scars the present: endemic violence a legacy of the civil war that ravaged Guatemala from 1960 to 1996. Torturing, kidnapping, murdering. The police, the military, the government as guilty as anyone. At the end of the war, an amnesty was granted for even the worst crimes. No one was accountable.

As bad as it is in Guatemala, it's far worse in Honduras — twice the murder rate of Guatemala. And El Salvador — three times. I'll have to pass through one of those on my route south to the Amazon, where I'll go balls deep into the depths of the jungle to drink ayahuasca, a sacred tribal brew. William S. Burroughs — the original ayahuasca tourist in the 1950s — said it was the strongest substance he'd ever experienced. "It is like nothing else," he said. "This is not the chemical lift of C, the sexless, horribly sane stasis of junk, the vegetable nightmare of peyote, or the humorous silliness of weed ... This is insane overwhelming rape of the senses ... It is space-time travel ... You make migrations, incredible journeys ..."

Should I be in Guatemala? Should I be journeying overland to the Amazon through savage states so I can take the most powerful hallucinogenic known to man?

Yes. Dare to roll the dice, I say; risk a one for a six. And it's a story to tell. Life should be about stories. "So, anyway, this one time a narco shot me ..." What a shame, what a waste, to be sat in the old farts' home and have little to reminisce, be short on tales to tell.

"Grandpa," says Little Johnny, "tell me about your life."

"I worked in an office for fifty years. At weekends, I went shopping, I watched TV, I drank beer."

"Is that it?"

"Err, let me think ... oh, and I married your nan ... and nine years later, we divorced."

"Anything else?"

"No, that's all, basically."

"Oh," says Little Johnny, frowning. "Will my life be like that?"

"Your life, Little Johnny, will be different. You can be anything, do anything. If you want, you can be a pirate. A princess, if you prefer."

Then they hit eleven, start at big-boy school, and the bubble is popped. Dreams of being an astronaut are no longer tolerated. "Be an accountant, Little Johnny; that's where the money is, that's what pays the mortgage."

And so it starts: A lifetime of slaving and saving for a life that never gets lived.

Plus, it's worthwhile to disappear now and then, to go AWOL from reality for months: in your absence, friends and family remember only your finest qualities; they forget your faults, forgive your wrongs. It's almost as if you've died. On your return, the red carpet is rolled, and you're treated like the resurrection. But you have to disappear for at least half a year to places considered dangerous. A month in the Maldives won't do.

Out of Flores, a tropical landscape unblemished, as green and wild as Mother intended. The largest settlements barely stretch back from the road they straddle. Hardly a building is higher than a storey. Huts for homes, shacks for shops. Walls of wood; roofs of steel, of thatch. Some are concrete, bland and grey as the day they were built. Homes to be lived in, not looked at. To the residents, these communities are coloured and intricate, but what can I see in a passing second but that which is obvious, and what is obvious is poverty. It's more like India than Mexico. Mexico is more like the US than here. Breadline living, basic as can be, is the norm for Guatemalans: 55% live in poverty; 29% in extreme poverty, on less than £2 a day.

The road dead-ends at the bend of a river, the Rio de la Pasion. "Coban?" I ask the driver, the next town on the map.

He points over the river.

A motor canoe ferries me across. On the other side is Sayaxche, a town of dusty roads running at right angles, of bumpkin commotion and bumbling disorder. Vans come and go; none set for Coban — their destination known via a sign in the windscreen or the shout of the driver. There's no ticket booth, no timetables. Purgatorial waiting ensues. It could be an hour, could be three. I may end up sleeping in Sayaxche. This is travel: A series of faltering transitions. Uncertainty is what you sign up for.

After a time, a driver breaks from yelling a destination that begins with R to ask me where I'm going.

"Coban," I tell him.

He doesn't understand.

I tell him again.

He still doesn't understand but tells me to get in the van. I get in.

Coban doesn't begin with R, but I don't have to go to Coban. What is it to me but a strange name on a map? On this journey of long-distance aimlessness, wherever I am is where I'm meant to be. Each place is as worthy as any other. So on I go, on the move towards an uncertain destination, a destination that's only a destination until it's reached; then it becomes a departure.

After two hours, the van stops at a crossroads. The driver tells me to get out.

"Here?" I ask, gesturing at nothing. We're not in a town, not even a village.

"*Si*," he says, and more I don't comprehend.

I get out, hope the part I didn't understand was that vans to Coban, or to somewhere, will drive by, pick me up.

A van does soon come, from the direction the previous one sped off to. It stops for me. "Coban?" I ask.

He nods.

It's packed beyond capacity, of course, but I jump on board anyway, not wanting to chance getting stuck at this spot. This van also has a cracked window; the difference is that it's the windscreen, the width of it. The interior panels are missing; the sliding door at times slides itself open. The only thing in good shape are the speakers — blasting eighties synth-pop. The driver's in a rush — they all are. He tries to overtake a truck on a bend, failing to see another oncoming at full throttle. Catastrophe narrowly avoided. He does the same again at the next bend.

This leg is on a remote stretch of road through Alta Verapaz, the greenest and wettest region in Guatemala, where on steep slopes sprout coffee and cardamon; through villages of indigenous communities where livestock wanders loose: flower-patterned blouses, flowing pleated skirts; babies stashed in slings on backs. Some sat like sages, stories written in their wrinkles; others at shacks, selling fruit. There a fellow riverside, panning for silver, perhaps gold. There one leading a donkey laden with firewood up a sinuous footpath to a lonesome building: a smoking chimney, holed linen strung on a line. The road rises and falls as it passes the densely-forested mountainscape — summits masked by mist. The rain just falls, obscuring the driver's view; as does the steaming of the windows. With the rain, the steam, the crack, and the stickers of Christ, visibility is 10%. The relentless downpour drenches bedraggled villagers who trudge roadside through muddy puddles that are fast forming streams, turning crater-sized potholes into swimming pools. None of the villagers carries an umbrella; a few use bin bags as cagoules.

Coban is drab, of no note; and Salama, the next stop, nondescript if you're generous, dreadful if you're not. A place to come to go, and the next place to go is the capital: Guatemala City. A bus this time, not a minivan; a so-called "chicken bus" to be precise: a decades-old school bus, a hand-me-down from Big Bro up north. At the end of their shelf life in the States, they're sent south for a new lease of life as a psychedelic-painted death trap. Besides a coat of paint, this one's jazzed with cuddly toys and a sound system that could hold its own in Ibiza. An eclectic playlist: sugary ballads to pulsing techno. Why bus drivers insist on playing dancefloor bangers, I don't know. No one on a bus wants to dance. What they spent on the sound system they should have spent on the suspension: my organs are rearranged. School children weren't meant to be driven at such speed. Haste to race ahead of other buses — to be first to pick up passengers — and also to thwart attacks: Gangs MS-13 and Barrio 18 govern here. They enforce extortion schemes; charges levied per bus per week. Pay or die. Passengers are at risk as well, which is why the UK Government's official foreign travel advice for Guatemala includes: "Avoid travelling on public buses (repainted US school buses)." To curb the gangs, police pickup trucks with swivel-mounted weaponry patrol; I saw them in Mexico, and I see them here; those aboard wearing commando-type combat gear, eyes barely visible through balaclavas.

The sun has set by the time I reach Guatemala City. A murder rate fifty times that of London. And even that is understated: The police don't count it as a homicide if a victim leaves the crime scene alive but later dies from the injuries. I want to hop on a bus to Antigua, 45 km away, but this is the northern bus terminal, and all the buses here go only north — where I've just come from. I ask at the information counter about hotels near the station. They say there are none, that I need to get a bus to the city centre. I board the bus they tell me to, the *Transurbano*; the others on board are mainly blokes, expressions chiselled to fuck-you. Outside, a teeming dystopia: Scummy suburbs sprawl, dimly-lit shantytowns tacked onto slopes, run-down buildings, rusting vehicles. Septic streets of chain-link fences and graffitied shutters, of scattered garbage and strewn liquor bottles. Heads pop up and peer, then quickly disappear, like urban whack-a-mole. Sinister weasels scuttle between cinder block boxes, skulk in the shadows. The discarded destitute fester: Rows of tents, ripped and stained, for block after bleak block; also dens and tarps and lean-tos, soiled mattresses and filthy, threadbare furniture.

I'm close to panic: One of the deadliest cities in the world, and I'm riding a bus at night, no idea where I am.

Half an hour passes with me staring through the mucked window at signs that don't speak to me, thinking I can't get off here, or here, or here. I'm still hoping for a Starbucks or McDonald's — something that signals it's a safer spot than others — when the bus stops and everyone gets off. It's the last stop. No choice but to walk, but to where? Asking randoms where to go will show my hand, out me as lost and alone to them and anyone around. Fine in a rural town in the day, not in a homicide hotspot at night. If I hail a taxi, he'll ask *which* hotel, and I'll say *any* hotel, and he'll think I'm a mug ripe to rob. And he'd be right. So I stand on a corner and look up the four streets, assess which has the most life, and walk down that one. I do the same again, and again, and again, follow the flow of people; past beat-up buildings and glowering doorways and gutters choked with trash and shops that have their fronts barred like cells; past scraggy mutts and scrawny children in scruffed clothes, their glassy eyes focused on the faraway. Hustlers and hawkers accost, alcoholics stagger and slur. Some curled up on flattened cardboard boxes beneath boarded-up windows; some wrapped head-to-toe in blankets, looking like body bags. The vibe is gnarly, and I'm a beacon. The stares speak, but there are words too: "Faggot," someone shouts. Street stalls take up a chunk of the sidewalk, causing knocks and bumps. I brace for a brush of the pocket, the sly steal; ball my hand in a fist, ready to strike. Twice I'm asked for money; one moves his hand down the back of his jeans. A knife, an itch: I don't wait to ask; I run.

I see a hotel — Hotel Reforma — as shite as a hotel can be; I head for it. In the foyer is a waterless fountain; a Christmas tree, somehow wilted even though it's plastic. The room is a film set for a suicide. A lightbulb blinks sallow light on a soiled bedsheet, a 2009 calendar hangs. Television bolted down; toilet roll holder padlocked. Through papier-mache walls: voices, music, horns, dogs, and the dull thud of a football being kicked — at one point, a hellish scream. Anything, though, at this time, will do. If all they had free was a dog basket in the backyard, I'd say, "Looks great; which corner do I crap in?"

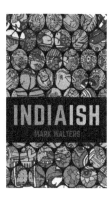

Mark rides buses and trains across Himalayan mountains and Rajasthani deserts; to super-cities like Delhi and Mumbai; and sacred spots like Varanasi and Rishikesh. He sees bodies barbecued beside the Ganges, goes insane when he drinks bhang lassi, visits the cult of "The Mother" ...

www.gonzo.schule/indiaish

RISHIKESH

Within the shitcake I've been eating, Rishikesh is a sweet, glazed cherry. Nestled in the forested foothills of the Himalayas, the Ganges bisects the town, and flows fresh from the mountains, free of faeces and corpses. On its banks, bells ring and chants float from colourful, ancient temples; ensconced within are *sadhus* and pilgrims, praying and prostrating, searching for salvation.

It's famed for being the cradle of yoga. Now hippie types flock to the town, the faithful and the freaks shopping in India's spiritualism supermarket. They join the locals meditating and contorting beside the sacred river. The guys try very, very hard; to impress the ladies, I suspect, because there are no bars or clubs in this town. Being able to perform a flawless Macarena under the influence of a dozen Jager-bombs holds no sway here. Unless a guy can touch his toes — without bending his knees — and talk about *kundalini* for fifteen minutes, he has no chance of getting laid.

Around town, every shop and cafe has included a New

Age word in their name — Freedom or Babylon or Krishna. Pinned to noticeboards inside are headshots of people purporting to be masters but who are patently muppets. The services advertised are manifold: reiki healing, tarot readings, trilotherapy sessions, consciousness maps, spiritual awakening — to name only a few. The one offering, "A journey into the time tunnel through soul molecule activation to appear in different time-space realities of human history," isn't a joke.

I had thought to spend a week in one of Rishikesh's many ashrams; places where you live a monk-like existence and spend all day doing yoga and meditating and sweeping floors. They're part fat camp — for people who have piled on mental rather than physical weight — and part cult, where you bare your spiritual hole for a bearded bloke to poke. It turns out, however, that International Yoga Week is next week, and so all the ashrams are booked up with people perfecting their postures and poses. But I'll still get my yogic groove on via some drop-in classes.

I've never tried yoga, but I may be a yoga person who just doesn't yet know it. I like tofu, I like whales, I like sitting down — the signs are there. I decided I'd need yoga pants and went to a shop earlier for that purpose, but when there I couldn't go through with buying some. I tried a few on, looked in the mirror, and thought I looked ridiculous. Every pair was so misshapen that even Krusty the Clown would deem them too ludicrous. So I'll attend the classes wearing jeans; the only jeans I have: skinny black ones.

The classes I've signed up for are at the Himalayan Yoga Retreat, which has a studio with a glass wall that looks out onto the Ganges flowing down from the Himalayas. The first class is Pranayama, a type of breath yoga that incorporates chanting. The instructor, Swami Prakash, looks like Jesus — if Jesus was Indian and sponsored by Tango. Only one other attendee, who resembles Thierry Henry in his Arsenal prime. Swami and Thierry have some rapport; he's evidently a regular attendee.

We sit cross-legged on yoga mats; me beside Thierry and Swami facing us, a couple of metres away. Swami mumbles something I don't catch because of bells ringing outside, and then they both, with eyes closed, start a ten-second-long, synchronised, "*Ommmmmmmmm.*" I join in on the second and subsequent rounds of it. My voice range doesn't go very deep: They're doing Stevie Wonder "*Ommmmmmmmms*", while mine are more Bee Gees: "*Ommmmmmmmm*, staying alive, staying alive, *ommmmmmmmm*, staying alive, staying alive."

After some sitting in silence, Swami says we'll do a some-thing-or-other chant. "I haven't got a printout to give you," he tells me. "Just listen and try to join in when you think you've got it." I listen intently to the random sounds they make, none of which are recognisable as words. It's on par with singing karaoke in Chinese. I keep quiet most of the time but chuck in the odd "uh" or "ah" now and again to let them know I'm still involved.

We do some breathing equivalents of rubbing our stomach while patting our head, then move on to something else I don't catch the name of: I have to rest my left hand on my knee and adopt a Trekkie gesture with the right, which I use to block one nostril while inhaling through the other. "Slower, slower," Swami tells me, as I hoover up air as one would a line of cocaine.

The next class — Hatha Yoga — starts straight after the first has ended. Three more people join us — looking-the-part twenty-somethings who will one day have kids with names like Peace or Sky. For five minutes, we sit with our knees floored and our bodies angled back over our bent toes. It's supposed to be a comfortable relaxation posture, but my knee joints are in pain. I'm grimacing; everyone else is smiling.

What follows is a super intense session of what is effec-tively a game of Simon Says ...

"Simon says lay on your front, with your hands in front of you, and arch your back."

"Simon says put your legs apart, with both heels on the floor, and bend low to your right side."

"Simon says put your right foot in front of your head, your left foot behind your back, and flap your arms like a chicken."

The kid in PE class at school who had no hope, like the

lard-arse running cross-country, or the wheelchair boy doing the high jump, today I am him. If it weren't for my earnest, pained face, Swami would think I'm taking the piss.

"Your heel isn't on the floor," he says. "Get your bottom down ... What's that hand doing there? ... No, *over*, not under ... Keep your mouth closed ... You're *inhaling*, not exhaling ..."

My ears are working; I know what I should be doing. It's the rest of me that's not working. My body just won't bend that way or that far. It's not my fault — it's genetics: my Dad has had both knees and hips replaced. I'm built from shoddy materials.

Swami eventually concedes that I'm as much a lost cause as a eunuch attempting the Kama Sutra. He starts giving me separate instructions to everyone else: "Everyone do x, y, z. Except you," and he points at me. "You just stand there and put your hands on your head."

Next comes pairwork exercises, and I get paired with Thierry. We lock limbs and push and pull each other; the result is something between a UFC match and recreations of erotic Italian sculptures. Thierry is, of course, better at the exercises than me. I'm complicating what would otherwise be easy for him. We're like Siamese twins, where one is in good shape but has an extra head and random limbs awkwardly attached.

When Swami tells us to take a rest, I assume it's the halfway point. I lay there looking like Stephen Hawking, wishing I'd prepared a contingency plan for this, as a debacle was always on the cards considering I haven't even jogged since 2014. If only I'd forged a note from my Mum saying I need to leave early for a doctors appointment. Shiva shows mercy on me, though: it's the end of the class.

It would be wrong of me to say yoga is a sham, nothing more than a ploy to shift excess stock of clown pants after the demise of circuses. I tried my best, but it wasn't a fair test on the merits of the practice. The test needs to be redone by someone more flexible than a plank of wood.

After a few hours interlude, I return to the scene of my yoga crime for something which should be simple: a class on meditation and mindfulness. Swami arrives ten minutes late;

he says he forgot there was a class at this time. I don't know how much confidence I can have in a mindfulness teacher forgetting about his own class on mindfulness.

No one else has come for the class, so I'm one-on-one with him. After we sit, he starts with a warning: "You must know that meditating can bring up feelings of misery, despair, loneliness."

I think: That might explain the one-man attendance.

He says we'll work through some techniques he developed during a several-month stint in a cave in the snowy Himalayas. He has me huffing and puffing, moving my chin up and down, and adopting peculiar positions with my arms.

For the last technique, he tells me to lay on my back with bent knees and make a noise that sounds like "shoe" on every inhale and a "ha" noise on every exhale: "Shoe haaaaaaa, shoe haaaaaaa, shoe haaaaaaa …" He leaves the room while I do this, and I lay there alone for fifteen minutes keeping it up: "Shoe haaaaaaa, shoe haaaaaaa, shoe haaaaaaa …"

When he comes back — by which time I can "shoe haaaaaaa" like a pro — he tells me to stop and lay there quietly with my eyes closed. As I lay there, I feel a warmth that starts in my toes rise slowly up through my body. I think: This malarky actually works: I'm a believer!

Then he says it's the end of the class and to open my eyes, and I open them to see he's put a portable heater by my feet.

In the evening, I attend a talk by a guru — Shri Prashant — at the Tree House Ganga Cafe. Three times today, I've been given flyers for the talk. The flyers declare Shri Prashant the founder of the Advait Movement and make a couple of bold claims: "The purpose of Advait is for the creation of a new humanity through intelligent spirituality." And: "His unique spiritual literature is on a par with the highest words that mankind has ever known."

The room the talk is held in is made from bamboo and wicker. Shri Prashant sits at the front on a cushion throne. He wears a yellow scarf and tracksuit bottoms and woolly socks. His appearance and demeanour are that of a baddie in *Scooby-Doo*; one who plots for world domination but is scuppered by meddling kids and their dumb dog. He's very precise about how the room is set up: no one can sit on a chair and no one can sit next to anyone they know — and he also says all phones have to be handed in and that we can't leave until the end. One guy walks out on hearing he can't have a chair. Everyone else — about thirty of us — sits on mats in a compact semi-circle around Shri Prashant.

He has half a dozen assistants. They were the ones handing out flyers earlier, and now they scurry about as per his commands. He gets them to give out double-sided A4 sheets printed with Bible teachings. He asks us to read the handouts then he sets about roasting Jesus, picking holes in the teachings. "Don't focus on the prophets of the past," he says. "Those like Jesus come and go. You need to be open to new prophets and know that they may have a different appearance to previous ones. Open your eyes; you're missing what's in front of you."

I think he means the latest prophet is Indian and wears woolly socks.

What he says over the next hour is wishy-washy; spiritual-sounding but lacking structure and specifics. If someone questions his nonsense, he closes them down and tells them they don't understand, that they're "scared of the truth". But many in the room have glazed expressions and hang off his every word. Some make notes — me too. I worry Shri Prashant will see me writing and ask me to share my thoughts. I don't want to read aloud that I've written I think he looks like a villain from *Scooby-Doo*.

Ninety minutes in — and by now a few have walked out — Shri Prashant goes nuclear: "I'm not going to sugar coat it. The people closest to you are those who will prevent your progress along the path. Do not stay attached to the false family of mother or father, brother or sister, husband or wife. They lead you astray from the truth. Leave them all behind for a new dynamic family. It is the only way for your salvation."

He eases off a bit after this with some random tangents, including five minutes on how squirrels live and what we can learn from their squirrelly ways. I mostly agree with his thoughts on squirrels.

I want to stick around to the end of the talk to catch the final hard sell and maybe get a free keyring, but my brain cracks three hours in after a twenty-minute back-and-forth about using the word "gain" in a spiritual context. I spring to my feet and make a dash for it.

Having Shri Prashant as my only Facebook friend would put a stop to endless baby photos in my feed, but I can't justify ditching everyone I know for a bloke that I share some common ground with regarding squirrels.

He's not the only one in town with a messiah complex. I've seen many wannabe messiahs here — both Indians and foreigners — walking around barefooted with feral hair flowing over their baggy tunics. They must be kept apart; friction is inevitable when they meet ...

"I'm the messiah."

"No, *I'm* the messiah. *You're* just a long-haired chump who can't afford shoes."

"Your mum's a long-haired chump who can't afford shoes."

"I have no mum. I was sent to earth by Brahma."

"Then who's that woman with the same surname as you who's the only one that follows you on Twitter?"

"Screw you, Dave."

"I'm not Dave; I'm Davarius."

"Your name's Dave, and you're a dickhead."

Fisticuffs follow; some scratching, a bit of hair pulling. Then they part; one to yoga class, the other to the time tunnel.

mark@gonzo.schule

www.gonzo.schule

Printed in Great Britain
by Amazon